The Catholic Imagination

The Catholic Imagination

Practical Theology for the Liturgical Year

SKYA ABBATE

RESOURCE *Publications* · Eugene, Oregon

THE CATHOLIC IMAGINATION
Practical Theology for the Liturgical Year

Copyright © 2012 Skya Abbate. All rights reserved. Except for brief quotations in critical publications or reviews, no part of this book may be reproduced in any manner without prior written permission from the publisher. Write: Permissions, Wipf and Stock Publishers, 199 W. 8th Ave., Suite 3, Eugene, OR 97401.

Resource Publications
An Imprint of Wipf and Stock Publishers
199 W. 8th Ave., Suite 3
Eugene, OR 97401
www.wipfandstock.com

ISBN 13: 978-1-62032-051-8
Manufactured in the U.S.A.

All scripture quotations, unless otherwise indicated, are taken from *The New American Bible*. New York: Catholic Book Publishing Co. 1992, 1987, 1980, 1970 and *The Catholic Study Bible*. 2nd ed. Ed. Donald D. Senior and John J. Collins. Oxford: Oxford UP, 2006.

Photos courtesy of Skya and Anthony Abbate.

All photos are of the Cathedral Basilica of St. Francis of Assisi in Santa Fe, New Mexico with the exception of the picture of Assisi Environment envisioned by the St. Francis Altar Society, Skya Abbate, President

To Mary and Anthony

Contents

Preface xvii
Acknowledgments xxi
Foreword xxiii

1 Advent and the Christmas Season 1

An Overview 2

The Liturgical Environment:
    Adveniat regnum tuum—thy kingdom come 2

Advent Awareness: Truly, this was the son of God! (Matt 27:54) 3

Mary in Advent: Blessed is the fruit of thy womb, Jesus 5

Gaudete Sunday, Advent Anticipation and Atonement:
    Lord, your love reaches to the heavens, your fidelity to the clouds (Ps 36:6) 6

Repentance and *Gaudete* Sunday: Rejoice and be glad
    (Alternative version) 7

Advent Adoration: For in the day of trouble he will conceal me
    in his tabernacle (Ps 27:5) 8

Christmas: Today salvation has come to this house (Luke 19:9) 10

Advent Arrival: Christmas—You are my son; this day I have
    begotten you (Acts 13:33) (Alternative version) 11

**2 Special Supplement for Advent and Christmas I:
Being with John 13**

Introduction: Being with John 14

The First Sunday of Advent: His name is John (Luke 1:63) 14

The Second Sunday of Advent: He must increase, but I must decrease (John 3:30) 15

The Third Sunday in Advent: John was a lamp that burned and gave light (John 5:35) 16

The Fourth Sunday of Advent: Behold, the Lamb of God (John 1:36) 18

3 **SPECIAL SUPPLEMENT FOR ADVENT AND CHRISTMAS II: THE WORD OF GOD IN THE OLD TESTAMENT FOR ADVENT—CHRIST, THE NEW CREATION** 21

Introduction: The Word of God in the Old Testament for Advent—Christ, the New Creation 22

The First Week of Advent: The Book of Genesis 1–3 23

The Second Week of Advent: Abraham and Election in Genesis 24

The Third Week of Advent and *Gaudete* Sunday: The Book of Exodus 26

The Fourth Week of Advent: Prophets and The Book of Kings 28

Christmas—O wondrous fidelity! Christ, the New Creation 29

4 **THE CHRISTMAS SEASON AND PRE-LENT ORDINARY TIME** 32

An Overview 32

The Feast of the Holy Family: By the power of the Holy Spirit he was born of the Virgin Mary and became man 32

The Feast of the Holy Family: Honor thy father and thy mother (Alternative version) 33

New Year: The one who does justice will live in the presence of the Lord 35

The Feast of the Solemnity of the Blessed Virgin Mary and the Feast of the Epiphany: The mighty one has done great things for me and holy is his name (Luke 1:49) (Alternative version) 36

The Most Holy Name of Jesus and the Feast of the Epiphany:
O come let us adore him (Alternative version) 37

The Feast of the Baptism of the Lord: Go therefore and make followers of all nations, baptizing them in the name of the Father, and of the Son and of the Holy Spirit (Matt 28:19) 39

The Feast of the Baptism of the Lord: Consubstantial with the Father 40

The Feasts of St. Paul, St. Thomas Aquinas and St. Francis de Sales: We are writing you this so that our joy may be complete (1 John 1:4)
January 25, 28 and 29 respectively
(May be during Lent) 41

The Feast of the Presentation of the Lord in the Temple: God from God, Light from Light
February 2 43

Our Lady of Lourdes and World Day of the Sick: Master the one you love is ill (John 11:3)
February 11 (May be During Lent) 44

The Feast of Saints Cyril, Methodius, and Valentine: Go out to the world
February 14 (May be During Lent) 45

5 **LENT AND EASTER** 47

An Overview 48

Fasting, Abstinence, and Almsgiving: But when you give alms, do not let your left hand know what your right is doing, so that your almsgiving may be in secret (Matt 6: 3–4) 48

Ash Wednesday: Come back to the Lord with all your heart; leave the past in ashes (Joel 2:13) 49

Ash Wednesday: Why are you so downcast my soul, why do you groan within me? (Ps 42:6) (Alternative version) 51

Lent and Environment: Lord send out your Spirit, and renew the face of the earth (Responsorial psalm based on Ps 104:30) 52

The Liturgical Environment for Lent: For with you is the fountain of life and in your light we see light (Ps 36:10) (Alternative version) 54

Lent and Prayer Through the Lens of Mark and Paul: I have seen the Lord (John 20:18) 55

The Scriptures of Lent: The Word of the Lord. Thanks be to God 56

Lenten Prayer: Forever I will sing, the goodness of the Lord (Responsorial psalm based on Ps 89:2) 57

Lent and Fasting: They tested God in their hearts by demanding the food they craved (Ps 78:18) 59

The Catechumens and the Liturgy: Whom are you looking for? (John 20:15) 60

Baptism: I am the Living Water (John 4:11) 61

Lent and Almsgiving: Give them what you have . . . I will take care of everything else that is needed (Mark 6:37) 62

Lent and the Oils of Our Faith: Go up to Gilead, and take balm (Jer 46:11) 63

The Chrism Mass and the Holy Oils: For I, the Lord, am your healer (Exod 15:26) (Alternative version) 65

Faith in the Desert: Her deserts he shall make like Eden, her wasteland like the garden of the Lord (Isa 51:3) 66

Laetare Sunday: *Laetare* Jerusalem, O be joyful Jerusalem 67

Laetare Sunday and the Feast Days of Lent—the Annunciation and the Feast of St. Joseph: Rejoice and be glad, yours is the kingdom of God (John 5:12) (Alternative version) March 25 and 19 respectively 68

Palm Sunday and the Triduum: And I will raise you up
on the last day (John 6:40) 69

Palm Sunday: What then is this that even the wind and the sea
obey? (Mark 4:41) (Alternative version) 70

Holy Week—The Passion, Death, and Resurrection: Father,
into your hands I commend my spirit (Luke 23:46) 72

Easter: He raises the needy from the dust (1 Sam 2:8) 73

6 SPECIAL SUPPLEMENT FOR LENT AND EASTER I:
FRANCIS FOR LENT 75

An Overview 76

Ash Wednesday and Almsgiving 76

The First Sunday of Lent—Suspension and Surrender 77

The Second Sunday of Lent—The Incarnation and Fasting 79

The Third Sunday of Lent—Rebuild my House 81

The Fourth Sunday of Lent—Chiara, Mary, and Creation 82

The Fifth Sunday of Lent—Islam, May the Lord
Give You Peace 84

The Sixth Sunday of Lent—Palm Sunday and the Stigmata 85

Easter and the Gospel: And it is in dying that we are born
to eternal life 87

7 SPECIAL SUPPLEMENT FOR LENT AND EASTER II:
LEARNING MARK BY HEART IN LENT 89

Week 1 Ash Wednesday 90

Week 2 John and Demons 91

Week 3 Healing and Blindness 92

Week 4 Peter 94

Week 5 Markan Parables 95

xii   Contents

      Week 6 Discipleship 96

      Week 7 The Holy Spirit 98

      Week 8 Easter in Mark 99

8 The Fifty Days of Easter, Special Feast Days and Saints 101

      Divine Mercy Sunday: Mankind will not have peace until it turns to the fount of my mercy 102

      Divine Mercy Sunday: Your mercy knows no bounds (Alternative version) 103

      The Feasts of St. Anselm and St. Mark the Evangelist: For a little time give your time to God, and rest in Him for a little (Anselm's *Proslogium*)
      April 21 and 25 respectively (May be during Lent) 104

      World Day of Prayer for Vocations and the Feast of St. Joseph the Worker: But the plan of the Lord stands forever (Ps 33:11)
      Fourth Sunday of Easter and May 1 respectively 105

      The Feast of Our Lady of Fatima: My Immaculate Heart will never abandon you (Fatima revelation)
      May 13 107

      Special Topic—St. Damien Joseph de Veuster of Moloka'i: Belgian, Hawaiian, and American Saint—I am a leper, blessed be the good God (Damien)
      May 10 108

      The Feast of the Ascension: I will see you again and your hearts will rejoice and no one will take your joy away from you (John 16:22) 110

      Pentecost: Receive the Holy Spirit (John 20:22) 111

9 ORDINARY TIME RESUMES 113

The Feast of the Most Holy Trinity: Glory be to the Father
 and to the Son and to the Holy Spirit 114

The Solemnity of the Most Holy Body and Blood of Christ
 (Corpus Christi): This is my body, which will be given
 for you (Luke 22:19) 115

The Feast of the Sacred Heart of Jesus and the Feast of the
 Immaculate Heart of Mary: Then he said to his disciple,
 'Behold, your mother" (John 19:26) 116

The Nativity of St. John the Baptist: *Ecce Agnus Dei*—
 Behold, the Lamb of God! (John 1:29)
 June 24 118

The Feast of St. Thomas the Apostle: My Lord and My God!
 (John 20:28)
 July 3 119

The Feast of St. Benedict of Nursia: *Ecce! Labora!* Go and work!
 (Benedict)
 July 11 120

Blessed Katerie Tekawitha and the Feast of St. Bonaventure:
 O good fortune!
 July 14 and 15 respectively 122

The Feast of St. James the Greater, Apostle: Son of Thunder
 July 25 123

The Feasts of St. Ignatius Loyola and St. Alphonsus Liguori:
 Give me Jesus Christ
 July 31 and August 1 respectively 124

The Transfiguration of the Lord and the Mystical Body of Christ:
 I have given you a model to follow so that as I have
 done for you, you should also do (John 13:15) 126

The Feast of the Assumption of the Blessed Virgin Mary
 into Heaven: *Theotokos!* Mother of God
 August 15 127

Special Topic—Indian Market and the Native American Liturgy:
All is fashioned by your hand 128

The Feasts of Saints Monica and Augustine: The path is not long
from your heart to God (St. Augustine)
August 27 and 28 respectively 130

The Feast of the Nativity of the Blessed Virgin Mary and the
Feast of the Most Holy Name of Mary: Hail Mary, Full
of grace, the Lord is with thee
September 8 and the First Sunday
after her nativity respectively 131

The Feast of the Exaltation of the Holy Cross:
Behold the wood of the cross
September 14 132

The Feast of St. Vincent de Paul: Care for each other,
I have cared for you
September 27 133

The Feast of the Archangels: Behold the Angel of the Lord
September 29 135

The Feast of St. Francis of Assisi: The Joy of Holy Poverty
October 4 137

The Feast of Our Lady of the Most Holy Rosary:
Preach my rosary
October 7 139

The Feast of St. Luke the Evangelist: Luke is the only one
with me (2 Tim 3:11)
October 18 140

The Feast of St. Paul of the Cross: May the Passion
of Jesus Christ be always in our hearts
October 19 141

The Feast of All Saints and All Souls Day: The Communion
of Saints, the Forgiveness of Sins
November 1 and 2 respectively 142

Dedication of the Basilica of St. John Lateran:
>   Our Mother Church
>   November 9 144

Dedication of the Basilicas of Saints Peter and Paul: Called
>   to be Apostles of Jesus Christ
>   November 18 145

The Feast Christ the King: and His kingdom will have no end 146

Glossary 149
Subject/Name Index 151

Preface

Let all things be blessed and holy, all is fashioned by your hand
MARTY HAUGEN, SONG AT THE CENTER

GOD CREATED THE WORLD and so the natural world is good. It has its seasons and nuances which shape our lives, mirroring, augmenting, enhancing, and making sacred the days of the year. The ecclesiastical calendar, marking the history and progression of our rich spiritual lives, consists of the themes and liturgies of the church's life. As co-creators in this journey we select, standardize, and share in the feasts, solemnities, sainthoods, and celebrations that constitute the liturgy of the Roman Catholic Church.

Year after year we repeat its familiar themes of Advent, Christmas, Lent, Easter, and Ordinary Time, and all the feasts and events that flow between them, becoming reawakened and renewed with their familiar rhythm, never tiring of their significance. As saints and songs have proclaimed, "Let heaven and nature sing." The presence of God permeates everything, but creation is unfinished. From Adam to us it is our responsibility to merge the secular with the sacred and share in the creation and fulfillment of the world. There is no need to rewrite or reinvent the Gospel or church history, only to reinterpret it in each historical time. Liturgy and liturgical reflection are ways to engender that action.

Meaningful worship and love of God are made complete by our committed presence and the "Catholic Imagination," a way of thinking, looking at, stimulating, and feeding our faith, our lives, and our response to God in concert with the seasonal and weekly themes of the liturgical year. In its simple, practical series of weekly lessons the reader is prompted to grow and mature by thinking about how their behavior can be a response to the timelessness of Gospel values and church tradition despite changing social times and mores. The reader is encouraged, by theological reflection, to coordinate their actions with the significance of the topic in the rhythm of the liturgical year and the natural world. Through reading, thinking, and discussion, the religious imagination is stimulated and structured so that the reader can act upon the wealth of their faith with committed presence and enter into an active relationship with God.

There is some freedom with liturgical planning for themes unique to each congregation to be practiced, such as music in Spanish or teen music, street processions or Indian dancers. These embellishments are allowed to involve the parish in their unique historical connection with God and to reflect their particular place in time and history. Yet the universality of the Mass, Holy Scripture and the liturgy of the Roman Catholic Church make it possible to worship God in a familiar way in every part of the world where the church is established. Not only language in the form of writings or songs, but the non-verbal symbols of behavior and environment such as established liturgical colors and symbols create a synergy important for the adoration of God, which is what liturgy is, "the work of the people." Liturgical elements for creating the church space in the form of environmental art through flowers, banners, colors and other elements, assist in focusing the lens of faith and conveying through symbol some of the grandeur and the mystery of God.

Many Catholics have not received the benefits of a formalized Catholic education as the basis of their faith, but even those who have leave the church, and of those who are faithful, many know very little about the scope of our shared history. Insufficient catechesis is cited as the leading reason why most people abandon their faith, so more instruction is certainly needed to retain and inform members, but in a manner that is relevant to their lives. Most catechesis comes from the pulpit at Sunday Mass and in effect that is very little. Reading Catholic books such as the Bible and *The Catechism of the Catholic Church* is an indispensable tool in the enrichment of faith, and yet few access the wealth of church literature. Simple little lessons and readings like this can go a long way in the continuing education of the lay Catholic with their straightforward message and inspirational topics that capture the faith and encourage reflection and action though discipleship.

This book begins with the liturgical year at Advent and goes through to the last Sunday of Ordinary Time, the Feast of Christ the King. Many topics pertain to the Sunday of the year, but the feasts of certain saints during some of the weeks are highlighted along with other church solemnities. The seasons of Advent, Christmas, Lent and Easter have alternative readings since these are such pivotal periods in the church year. Two focused supplements for Advent and Lent are included for deeper reflection on the Incarnation and the celebration of the focal point and apogee of our faith—the Paschal mystery. Some feasts have fixed dates determined by the church such as the Feast of the Solemnity of Mary on January 1. Other feasts are moveable such as the feast of Christ the King. Easter is the reference point for all the dates of each particular year.

This little book is suitable for lay members of the Roman Catholic Church, catechetical, pastoral, and liturgical ministers, and it stands independently as a private meditation book to be used throughout the liturgical year's journey, yet not limited to any one of the liturgical years A, B and C. As St. Benedict of Nursia proclaimed, "Let nothing be preferred to the work of God." That work is up to the Catholic imagination, a hermeneutic that engenders Catholic presence through Christian commitment. Enjoy the journey of our faith.

Acknowledgments

IN THANKSGIVING TO MY parish, the Cathedral Basilica of St. Francis of Assisi, my home in Santa Fe, New Mexico, the City of Holy Faith, for your spirit of love and community

To Sister Emilia Atencio for believing in me and gently nudging me to do things I never dreamed

To the members of the St. Francis Altar Society of the Cathedral Basilica of St. Francis of Assisi for your welcoming confidence and trust in me

To the Liturgy Committee of the Cathedral of the Basilica of St. Francis of Assisi for allowing me to find God in the discipline of the word, thought, and service, especially to Monsignor Jerome Martinez y Alire for your trust in allowing a simple person to write from faith to the parish

To Janis and John Gasparich, Mary Richman, Trish Byrd, Carrie Lynn Korzak, and my brothers and sisters, who have told me to write—your fidelity has sustained and inspired me.

Foreword

EXPANDING UPON HER BROAD yet deep educational base as a sociologist and doctor of Oriental Medicine, Skya builds upon exploring the richness of the human condition seen through the clearest of possible lenses, belief in Jesus Christ. Through her simple and poetic images, born from being an astute lover of nature and nourished by the beauty of the Southwest desert, her writing style effectively works for the short one-piece reflection pieces that describe the weeks of the liturgical year of the Roman Catholic Church. In easy to understand language she is able to capture the tradition and magisterial teachings of the church in concert with the particular weekly theme in ways the person in the pew and the pulpit can appreciate and act upon. Enriched by ministerial participation in her parish community and a life-long Catholic education, and now advanced degree studies at Loyola University, New Orleans, Skya is always seeking ways to convey the basics, diversity, and wisdom of our spiritual traditions. In this on-going endeavor to let people experience the joy of discipleship, and to recognize the faithfulness of God for all people, she keeps developing new essays that have now gone from the written word into practice. Through conducting ministerial retreats on her favorite topics—prayer, the Gospel of Mark, and the sacrament of the anointing of the sick, Skya describes herself as a practical, bottom-line person, and her faith as the core of a theology that likewise must be practical and put into action or it is meaningless.

In what is surely the first of many books to come, which will go into more depth on topics such as social justice, ecological theology, pastoral leadership skills, and the centrality of reconciliation and Eucharist as the heart of our shared faith, this little book initiates the reader into what Skya calls the "Catholic Imagination," a paradigm of looking at our everyday world through the hermeneutic of faith. It is a valuable small work that can be easily accessed and quickly read; yet hopefully the readings inspire the ongoing conversion and transformation into holiness that all of us are called to.

Since childhood Skya said she wanted to be a theologian and it seems the roads she has taken all in the pursuit of truth brought her back to her childhood faith. Surely that single-minded love of God in practice is the definition of a theologian.

The Reverend Monsignor Jerome Martinez y Alire, JCL
Rector, Cathedral Basilica of St. Francis of Assisi,
Santa Fe, New Mexico

1

Advent and the Christmas Season

The Advent Wreath over the baptismal font
and Mary as the center

AN OVERVIEW

Advent is that period of joyful anticipation that precedes Christmas and marks the beginning of the liturgical year. As the Western calendar comes to an end, the church year begins. Advent consists of the four Sundays and the time between that lead up to the great feast of Christmas, the nativity of Jesus. Consideration of Advent should encompass the liturgical environment, its Sundays and feast days, Gospels, and the hallmark themes of joyful anticipation, atonement, almsgiving, and adoration. Let us begin the journey of Advent that is beginning of the journey of our faith.

THE LITURGICAL ENVIRONMENT:
ADVENIAT REGNUM TUUM—THY KINGDOM COME

This week, the familiar liturgical environment of comforting green is transformed from the dual vibrancy and dryness of autumn to a new period of expectancy. It is the end of the calendar year but the beginning of the liturgical one as we await the coming of the Messiah. *Advent*, that special pre-Christmas period whose meaning is "to come," heralds both the birth of Christ in history, his Second Coming at the end of time, and his continual rebirth daily into our lives

Decoratively to crown this holy season is the Advent wreath, positioned variously in churches, suitably suspended over the baptismal font, the focus of our life in Christ, or over the altar, the rock of our salvation. All eyes turn to it at the start of Mass and when one enters the church. Simple yet regal, it is adorned with hopeful blue-violet and pink ribbons and candles, reflective of the winter skies and hopeful anticipation that will count down the weeks to Christmas and mark where we are in the preparation of our hearts for the joyous event of the nativity of Our Lord Jesus Christ.

The appropriateness of incense continues as a central liturgical element giving pleasing praise to God in its ascent. New aromas of rich balsam, pine and fir, along with frankincense and myrrh are introduced, reminiscent of ancient times when incense was a gift for kings and God. The verdant green vestments, banners, and altar cloths of the thirty plus weeks of Ordinary Time now change to a bluish purple distinguished from the darker reddish purple of Lent, embellished with symbols such as a radiant star or a candle, proclaiming this as special time of the light within the darkness. Words such as "O Come Emmanuel" or "Prepare Ye," may be proclaimed across them—words of hope and welcome or preparatory repentance needed to see God.

Gift giving starts now not just at Christmas. Baskets are stationed in the sanctuary, or entry or at the foot of the altar for offerings of food for the needy of our community. There is no holiday from hunger. Perhaps hunger and the discrepancies of wealth and poverty are more poignantly exacerbated at this time of celebration. Within God's house we can try to end it at least for a time during the season of giving, and recommit ourselves beyond the season to caring for these lowly who have an especial kinship with God.

The empty crib stationed beneath a crucified Christ, at the foot of the paschal candle, or the footsteps of the sanctuary invite us to meditate. He was born into the world to suffer and die for us. The cross is where the Christmas story is leading but it won't stop there for there is reason to hope. He came into the world to rise and give us life again by redeeming us from sin and restoring the right relationships between each other and God.

Just as the empty crib will be filled with the miracle of love of the Incarnation, we can fill it with the radiance and warmth of our belief, forgiveness, and love. Adorn it with baby food, blankets, diapers, and toys, gloves, hats, scarves and thermal clothing, socks and sweatshirts for the aged, or the needs of the community. Most of all, fill it with quiet joy, love, and yearning, gifts befitting Jesus and his presence in all, especially the little ones we must be to enter the kingdom of heaven.

ADVENT AWARENESS: TRULY, THIS WAS THE SON OF GOD!(MATT 27:54)

It is Advent. Something has changed. Our sense of self and possibility is renewed; hope has been restored. It is a time of waiting that requires patience. We anticipate the Second Coming of Christ just as the Chosen People awaited the Messiah. Perhaps we are not unlike them? Have we become impatient, complacent, like them? Do we want immediate gratification and are unwilling to sacrifice, suffer, pray and conform our lives to the Gospel? The choice is ours. We don't live in the time of the prophets like the Chosen People in the Old Testament. Revelation has become flesh. The kingdom of heaven is not light-years away.

One of the Advent Gospels of the liturgical year B belongs to Mark. In Mark there is no mention of the nativity. As the shortest of the Gospels, his message is urgent beginning with the announcements of John the Baptist. It is a Gospel of miracles, mystery, and the public ministry of the human and divine Jesus. Now is a good to read the Gospel of Mark. It is an opportunity to meet and listen to God through his word. Did you know that you can receive a partial indulgence for reading the Bible so as the venerate God, and a plenary indulgence if you read it for one half hour? Do we care about these indulgences anymore or only about our own personal indulgences?

The season of Advent is one of hopeful anticipation. John has leapt in his mother's womb. Mary awaits the holy birth of her son, and we remember the unborn who have been given the gift of life. Will we say yes to that miracle? Interestingly, the Feast of Our Lady of Guadalupe, Patroness of the Americas, and the unborn, is celebrated during this month too. Advent is a time of angelic proclamations. The angels have appeared to Mary and Joseph with the announcement that God will be made man and the angels will surround him at birth.

It is a season of actualization; a time for us to do some special things. The journey to Bethlehem is about to begin and it is not so far from Calvary. But first let us make room in the warmness of our hearts for the child that we will welcome at Christmas. We can make that room by emptying our hearts through atonement, almsgiving, and adoration. Then, offer up your emptiness, and like a Christmas stocking from a good father, it will be filled with more than we can imagine!

We may be more inclined to think of this time as the Christmas season than the Advent period. Christmas can bring lots of stress over traveling, preparing fancy meals, family gatherings, no money for gifts, and loss of loved ones. But the Advent season is hopeful, each week bringing us closer to God if we move methodically and trustfully in that direction. Begin Advent with awareness. Let the light from the Advent candles, the Gospel promise of Christ as the light of the world, and the pristine winter night make the important things clear to us.

> *An indulgence is a full or partial remission of temporal punishment due for sins that have already been forgiven. The church grants the indulgence after the sinner has confessed and received absolution.

MARY IN ADVENT:
BLESSED IS THE FRUIT OF THY WOMB, JESUS

Even as devote Catholics we can easily let the role of Mary become obscured in Advent with the cultural, commercial emphasis on Christmas. But throughout this time the church celebrates several important Marian feast days apart from her obvious role at Christmas as the mother of God. At the start of Advent two special feast days relevant to Mary in her capacity as a mother are commemorated—the Feast of the Immaculate Conception and the Feast of Our Lady of Guadalupe.

December 8, one of the Holy Days of Obligation, is the Feast of the Immaculate Conception of the Blessed Virgin Mary. This day recognizes Mary, the new Eve, as free from the stain of original sin from the moment of her conception, thus preparing her to become the mother of the Savior. December 12 is the Feast of Our Lady of Guadalupe. Between December 9 and 12 in 1531, on a hill in Tepeyac close to Mexico City, Mary appeared to now canonized peasant Juan Diego. In the midst of winter she filled his cloak with roses and left behind her image imprinted on its rough cactus fiber as proof to the bishop of her apparition, and her desire that a church be built here so that the one true God would be with the people of his country.

In this only approved Marian apparition in North America, Mary is likewise lauded though understatedly, as Patroness of the Americas. She is a saint for our continents, one we need to remind us of the importance and respect deserving to mothers of the living and the unborn. While we can never approach her unequivocal "yes" to be the mother of God, we can try to emulate her grace-filled acquiescence by honoring her as the protector of the immortal souls of the unborn, just as she agreed to protect the unborn Jesus.

Yearly, the children of our churches can delight in watching the statues of Mary and Joseph, if they are placed throughout the church and rearranged weekly, on their way to the crèche. We can make that trip with Mary too by invoking her for our needs—indeed she wants to be called on. Some saints call Mary "the short cut to God" for as his mother he can refuse her nothing.

When the weeks pass and the feasts of Mary are gone, let us remember her central role in salvation history. She carried Christ in pregnancy beneath the cathedral of heart. Her immaculate heart and his sacred one are entwined for all eternity. Our yearning hearts can be enmeshed with theirs as well if we allow our hearts to be awakened through love of Jesus, the Christmas rose, the light of the world, through his holy mother, our mother Mary.

GAUDETE SUNDAY, ADVENT ANTICIPATION AND ATONEMENT: LORD, YOUR LOVE REACHES TO THE HEAVENS, YOUR FIDELITY TO THE CLOUDS (PS 36:6)

Anticipation is mounting. Christmas is approaching. Will it be different this year? News reporters and financial experts say spending will be down and cutbacks will be made. Parents worry about gifts for the children that they feel define Christmas. "Should we get a new credit card to have a modest Christmas?" they call in to the nightly news shows. People discuss how they plan to make it different this year apart from cutting down on purchases. More hugs, sharing food, buying groceries for a poor neighbor, gathering together recounting stories, laughing at the good, and finding humor in the difficult are the resourceful and understanding answers.

We can be resilient because we were made in God's image and likeness even if we don't always mirror it. Maybe this can be a good old-fashioned Christmas when we aren't intimidated to say the words "Merry Christmas" out loud, when food, family, friends, and faith are the focus over fancy and frivolous gifts, when simplicity and genuine warmth can keep out the cold and warm us more than any new coat or fireplace.

This Sunday is *Gaudete* Sunday; the Sunday of rejoicing in the midst of Advent for the Good News is here. In the northern hemisphere the days are the very shortest, but in two weeks when winter arrives the days will become longer, almost a contradiction. Just as the sun with its light and warmth will slowly return, so does the hope of creation, the son of God. The church environment reflects this joy in the dawn colors of pink and white flower buds and dusky rose vestments. We are rescued from the darkness of sin and restored to the birthright God intended for us before we allowed sin to grip us. The pink candle of the Advent wreath that is lit this week blushes in anticipation. The ecclesiastical liturgy mirrors the liturgy of the natural world. Creation is fulfilled through the hope of Jesus Christ, his Second Coming, and as Henri Nouwen, priest and theologian reminds us, the meaning of the Incarnation is that God is the God of the present moment. So until Easter, stubborn buds and cold spring flowers will push through the frozen earth one last time, a silent, hopeful reminder of the life dormant in what appears to have perished. Buy a Christmas cactus, an amaryllis bulb, a paperwhite or an orchid and watch it bloom. That is the nature of life!

Christmas is soon. It is a good time to receive the sacrament of reconciliation whose forgiving, living grace will nourish the bud of life in the soul longing to be a full-blown blossom. Birth is just around the corner in confession, recommitment to the cross, and Christmas.

REPENTANCE AND *GAUDETE* SUNDAY: REJOICE AND BE GLAD (ALTERNATIVE VERSION)

The citywide or parish penance service may have passed or is coming up but it is never too late to go to confession. It is the Third Sunday of Advent—*Gaudete* Sunday—the Sunday of rejoicing. Small signs of life in spring flowers appear in the church, and uplifting rose-colored vestments, ribbons, and banners are displayed. The pink candle of the Advent wreath is lit. Have you noticed weekly that the Advent candles are lit from the Paschal candle, conferring the hope and promise that begins at Advent and will be fulfilled at Easter?

Have we emerged from the wilderness of our hearts and made "straight" the way of the Lord as St. John the Baptist exhorted? Are we ready for that divine moment in time when Christ came into the world for the first time on Christmas, and when he will come again? New life is possible. The sacrament of reconciliation is one way to reclaim that new life.

Statistics from the Center for Applied Research on the Apostolate at Georgetown University tell us that 42 percent of Roman Catholic Americans never go to confession, 14 percent go once a year, and only 2 percent go regularly. Respondents claim reconciliation is not effective or a meaningful practice for them, or that they rather pray directly to God. Many say they have lost confidence in confession due to the clergy scandal, but is that really a reason to shun a sacrament because some have fallen? Do we not need to practice reconciliation as part of our Catholic recommitment and on-going conversion to holiness? Is anything unforgivable? Even the thief on the cross in the last minutes of his life was promised paradise that day with Jesus.

Reconciliation is one of the seven sacraments. A sacrament is an institution ordained by Christ to give grace, that is, it confers what it signifies. He commissioned the apostles and their successors with the power to forgive. To ignore that is to ignore the will and the word of God. While personal prayer should be an integral, daily part of our life, a sacrament has its own special standing. We need to cultivate the conscience and the humility of an examined life, to reveal our sins and ask for forgiveness so we are reconciled to Christ and his body, the church. A sacrament is not just a religious or personal act but is a social one as well, for by the forgiveness of sin, our correct relationship with God and each other is restored. Reconciliation is the opportunity for conversion, the renewal of Baptismal commitments in a new time and situation. It empowers us so that we can go forward as flawed and gifted people, not just from the consolation it delivers, but also in the on-going increasing commitment that is requisite to being a follower of Christ.

Be part of the 2 percent! Experience the joy of *Gaudete* Sunday with joyful repentance. Receive the joy and healing mercy of Jesus through confession. Give yourself the Christmas gift of heartfelt confession and recommitment, and let Jesus give you one too—the gift of his forgiveness through the grace of sacramental reconciliation.

ADVENT ADORATION: FOR IN THE DAY OF TROUBLE HE WILL CONCEAL ME IN HIS TABERNACLE (PS 27:5)

The tabernacle is the soul and cornerstone of every Roman Catholic Church. It is a holy place, where the Body and Blood, Soul and Divinity of Our Lord Jesus Christ reposes day and night, day after day. That is quite a formidable, incomprehensible reality.

The first tabernacle of church history dates back to when on Mt. Sinai Moses received the Ten Commandments written on stone from God. Moses was then instructed by God to build the Ark of the Covenant, the prototype tabernacle that would house his word on the tablets of stone, signifying his presence, and the protection of his favored people. It also contained *manna*, the blossoming rod of Aaron, a gold vase, and other holy texts—all presages of the priesthood of Jesus Christ. Of gold and timber, the sacred chest called the Ark of the Covenant was constructed and carried in a tent surrounded by a cloud through which God spoke as it traveled with the nomadic Israelites in the desert until they reached Jerusalem. When the temple of Solomon was built, it found its last home. The temple was destroyed in 587 BCE at the fall of Jerusalem and the remains of the Ark were left unknown.

The transition of the tabernacle of wood to the flesh of Jesus began with Mary. This season we celebrate two Marian feasts, placed appropriately in the Advent period. The Feast of the Immaculate Conception honors Mary and her preservation from original sin. She is the holy temple who held our Lord in her womb. The Feast of Our Lady of Guadalupe commemorates the North American apparition of Mary to St. Juan Diego, promising to bring peace to the new world. She is both the Patroness of the Americas and of the unborn housed in the womb. Mary is referred to as the New Ark of the Covenant. That title denotes her role as the human tabernacle of God. This is another unfathomable mystery, that the Trinitarian God of eternity, in the manifestation of the son, was begotten in his mother's womb, to become like us.

In Catholic tradition the temple was no longer required. As Jesus died, the veil of the temple was split in two. Jesus said he would destroy the temple and raise it in three days, an idea no one could understand in connection to the literal Jewish temple of stone. But as we know Jesus was referring to his body that would die and then be resurrected in three days. We still need his presence, a tabernacle in our midst, and he left it to us in the Eucharist, so as to make us new tabernacles of his presence. He will be with us even until the end of the world.

He is with us in the tabernacle of the church too. Many tabernacles repose in the beautiful Blessed Sacrament chapels of our main churches. Today the tabernacle houses the Eucharist reserved for the sick, the Holy Communion not received from Mass, and the Blessed Sacrament for adoration. It is a golden box more marvelous than any Christmas gift, one that will never stop giving or delighting. We can visit our Lord in the tabernacle every day in contrast to churches in many parts of the world that may only be open once a week or even once a month. St. Alphonsus Liguori writes that it is a pleasing practice to spend time with Jesus Christ on the altar. We can talk to him about our troubles and fears and he will comfort us and surely it is true. This Advent, deflect the focus on the tree or the gifts, the lights or the food. The greatest gift of the world is with us in the tabernacle of our church and our hearts.

CHRISTMAS: TODAY SALVATION HAS COME TO THIS HOUSE (LUKE 19:9)

Christmas is almost here. Is there anyway to describe it—the magical excitement of childhood memories? Twinkling lights, the tinseled tree, sweet treats. Candy canes, crunchy wrapping paper, colorful ribbons. Waking up early, church, and carols. Food, family, friends. School vacation, special times. Santa, snow, the star in the darkness, the stockings that are hung. The nativity scene, gingerbread houses. The longing for gifts wanted, the expectation of something miraculous. Can we keep that expectancy alive as adults with our family, in our community, and in our church? Are we still waiting for that special gift we couldn't even verbalize, its need was so great, so deep, one we only know when we receive it? Can we feel the mystery of that holy night, that joyful day, that holiday season? Can we experience the fulfillment that only Christ, the light of the world, can give to our deep yearning?

The liturgical color for Christmas as well as most holy days is the white of the lamb and the glory of heaven. The church is ready with lush white or startling red poinsettias. Pink is proper for Mary. The bare aspens bow to the full Christmas tree. God's promise to humankind is fulfilled. Mary and Joseph have journeyed to Bethlehem to be counted in the census. It is a small town where there is no room for them at the inn. The town's name means "House of Bread." Bread, so basic, so fundamental, virtually every culture has an equivalent. And here Jesus is born, the bread of life who will give us his body to become the living bread of eternal life, the Eucharist. This is the meaning of the Incarnation, God stepping into human history as a newborn baby. He takes on our likeness as we took on his at creation.

At the eleventh hour, at midnight Mass or in the living room assembling a bike for a child, are we refreshed or weary from the season? Are we ready for our birth on this holy night when through the Incarnation, the *manna* from heaven is given to us forever, a never-ending gift that will make every Christmas everlasting. He is the star that showed the people of all nations the way to his love and peace when we welcome him into the inn of our hearts. O night divine, the advent of God in a child!

ADVENT ARRIVAL: CHRISTMAS—YOU ARE MY SON; THIS DAY I HAVE BEGOTTEN YOU (ACTS 13:33) (ALTERNATIVE VERSION)

On the gently sloping green the ecumenical Christmas service was about to begin. The lambs were sleepy, but still looking around for a little grass to nibble on, and the donkey, nervous to be so close to the sea, raised his eyes in supplication to heaven. The concelebrant, happy over the turnout of the local Jamestown residents on a cold winter's eve, couldn't restrain himself on the night of the birth of Christ and the start of the live nativity scene re-enacting that miraculous moment. He excitedly coaxed the crowd not to chastise him as he invoked them to turn to the east to witness the full copper moon kneeling in the purple night sky under the Newport Bridge and over the cold Atlantic Ocean. Here was the glory of creation making a dramatic appearance in reverence and proclamation for the birth of Christ.

Meanwhile, at St. Francis de Sales Church a few miles up the street, the Christmas Vigil Mass was about to begin. It was a beautiful special Mass overflowing with families and friends bundled close together, packing the church wall to wall in winter coats housing human hopes. At the start of the service, to the surprise of the assembly, the priest proclaimed that this year the Gospel would be both read and re-enacted.

At the appropriate time from the side of the sanctuary, a young family emerged dressed in clothes from the time of Jesus. They were ordinary and without ostentation. The new mother sat in the chair by the altar. The young father stood behind her in support. In her arms she held a new baby of perhaps only two months old. As the Gospel was read the woman held up the child. The baby looked downward, perfect, smiling, glowing, luminous.

The church was silent beholding him. He was truly the God in all of us, so pure, so innocent, so vulnerable and trusting. Time stood still. We were in the manger of the past, in the church now, in the heaven of the future. If only we could have stayed that way for all time, it might have been enough. If only we could see God in every living being from the time they were conceived, born, lived and died, and treated them that way, the world would be a different place, a reality only possible with the advent of God in our lives.

It was perfect moment, a silent night surprise, an extraordinary night when the God of creation simultaneously kissed the earth with his magnificent moon, bowed at his son's birth in the nativity scene, and raised him in his arms in the church in front of his faithful, all done in the holy silence of the night.

The baptismal font at Christmas

2

Special Supplement for Advent and Christmas I

Being with John

Advent banner with John's message

INTRODUCTION: BEING WITH JOHN

PERHAPS MORE THAN ANY person other than Mary, the Advent season belongs to St. John the Baptist. In this series in Advent, let us encounter whom Jesus said was the greatest of all men born of women so that we can deepen our understanding of the significance of the Incarnation in our lives. May we use this Advent period as a time of grace for the world and us.

THE FIRST SUNDAY IN ADVENT: HIS NAME IS JOHN (LUKE 1:63)

Born of a woman of advanced age considered barren and disgraced, and a man dumbstruck with disbelief over his son's conception, proclaimed by an angel, and filled with prenatal grace, John the Baptist came into the world. He was the cousin of Jesus, born six months earlier than Jesus, the last and greatest prophet, the precursor who would herald the Messiah. John first met his cousin in the womb when he leapt for joy at the visitation of his mother Elizabeth and Jesus' mother Mary. Who can doubt the sacredness of the unborn filled with the spirit of God? Blessed is the fruit of thy womb.

After his birth, at the time of his circumcision, when all expected him to be named after his father Zechariah, the mute father insisted that the child's name be John as was told by the angel Gabriel, the same angel who announced to Mary that she was chosen to be God's mother. "Yahweh is gracious, merciful," was the meaning of his name, and God certainly was beneficent with the gift of John to us.

Not much is known about this greatest of saints, which gives us hope that even in our anonymity we can be holy. Who can say that one person does not make a difference? Due to the age of his parents, he was probably raised in a community, but it is said that at an early age he retired to the desert for a period of preparation for his ministry. Art depicts him playing with his cousin Jesus, with Mary, and Elizabeth, and holding a lamb symbolic of Jesus and ritual sacrifice. The unusual painting of John shedding his everyday clothes to enter the wilderness is not unlike that of St. Francis of Assisi who cast off his rich garments to begin a new radical life of poverty when his father rejected him. Clothes apparently do make the man! John said if you have two cloaks give one away. Maybe we can share our abundant clothes with the poor and the homeless by giving them our warm, well-cared for garments this cold season, or even a new one!

All four Gospels in varying degrees begin with the birth, life, and the ministry of St. John the Baptist, an iconoclast by any standard. Mark's is the shortest and most dramatic, Luke's is the most detailed and longest. Matthew's is scholarly, John's perhaps the most beautiful, poetic, and prophetic. But all four evangelists recognized John's transitional role from Judaism to Christianity, from the rabbinical to the messianic era. John was alluded to in the Old Testament, referred to as Elijah who the Jews thought would forecast the Jewish rebellion from political control and who would deliver a corresponding earthly reward. But he was not Elijah come again but John, and he stripped himself of his clothes and his self. Can we relate to his essence of extrication from the world? John didn't waste time with the unimportant things. He had urgency, an intense longing for the life in Christ that we ache for. John is an incomparable gift, a gift from God to the world. How can we share our lives with others this Advent, and akin to John, recognize what and who is important?

THE SECOND SUNDAY IN ADVENT: HE MUST INCREASE, BUT I MUST DECREASE (JOHN 3:30)

The child grew and became strong in spirit and he was in the desert until the day of his manifestation to Israel. Emerging perhaps after ten years of being in the wilderness, at about the age of thirty, John the Baptist stations himself in the verdant Jordan Valley, along the Jordan River that flows into the Dead Sea. It is time for his ministry to be brought to fruition after a period of isolation, asceticism, and repentance. He spends his days in the fresh river water baptizing those who have already repented of their sins, and now complete their conversion in an external ritual of cleansing with running, living water.

The practice of Baptism seems to have been an historical Jewish rite, and an Essene one in particular, for the converts to the Jewish faith. John's Baptism was a logical and natural extension of such traditions and our understanding of water. But his rite could not compare with what Jesus would replace it with even though Jesus submitted to Baptism as a model for what we all need to do. It was also an opportune time for God the father to reveal Jesus as his son and his approval of his son's mission.

It was after Jesus' Baptism that Jesus' public ministry began and John recognized his own role now as less significant.

Just as the topography of the world has been carved from its great rivers, so too Baptism, as instituted by Jesus would henceforth mold our souls. We would belong to God, and those channels created by the sacrament, like rivers flowing with water, would be further conduits of his grace of friendship and love. John said Jesus would baptize with the Holy Spirit and fire, and the disciples, some of whom were with John and Jesus, came to understand this need for purification as they followed him from the cool waters of Baptism to the fire of his passion and Pentecost.

Today the Jordan River is drying up, its fresh water turning stagnant, not emptying into the Dead Sea to where it flows, its once lush valley dry and unproductive. The Dead Sea is becoming even saltier than it once was; crystal islands of salt are coalescing and reducing the body of water. How is the water of our Baptism running? Has it dried up like the Jordan, not feeding the environs around it? Or has our soul repeatedly collected the graces of the sacraments in our lifelong journey. We only need to be baptized once, but we do need a lifetime of repentance, conversion, and recommitted presence to perform the actions that follow from that repentance to keep us pure like running water, for we are not without sin, but we are saved.

Advent is only a short time but a perfect period to assess our time in the desert like John did, and to realize the consequence of sin and to turn away from it. The church environment is as stark as John's attire and our empty hearts. So rise above the comfortable status quo and receive the Sacrament of Reconciliation this month well before Christmas so that the feast will be lush with sacramental grace. As we lift up our voices without music, sing in John's plaintive, expectant voice—O come, O come Emmanuel. Jesus and John are closer than you think. The kingdom of heaven (God) is at hand.

THE THIRD SUNDAY IN ADVENT: JOHN WAS A LAMP THAT BURNED AND GAVE LIGHT (JOHN 5:35)

Herod the ruler of Galilee, who feared a political uprising that the Jews also expected from a new leader, soon arrested the private recluse turned popular and passionate prophet, preaching about the imminence of a new order and salvation from sin. While he was imprisoned, the disciples went to John to attest that Jesus was the one who was greater than he, and John confirmed that he was not fit to fasten Jesus' sandal. John further angered Herod by condemning his adultery with his brother's wife, Herodias. When her daughter Salome performed a seductive dance pleasing to Herod, he promised her whatever she desired. Upon consultation with her mother, Salome demanded the head of John the Baptist on a platter immediately, and so John was martyred by being beheaded, an act even Herod knew to be unjust.

Herod's rash public oath, which he did not recant even though he did not want to murder John, reminds us also to watch our words in public. Do not boast, do not say what you don't mean to follow through on or have the courage to change if you make a mistake. More importantly do not do anything that brings down the body of Christ. When New Year comes we will all probably make some resolutions rather rashly as well. While we may be well intentioned it is hard to change behavior overnight. That is why the period of Advent is so beautiful for it is exactly that, a time of preparation for behavioral change and slow conversion. It is the true beginning of the year, the liturgical year, so it is a good time for resolutions that can be made over time. While it is not a forty day period that we are used to in Lent, in the ark or the desert or the belly of the whale, it is similar to those periods of preparation. Christmas like Canaan is the goal. We can get there only because God has gone ahead of us in Jesus.

Our themes or "resolutions" of Advent should be prayer, almsgiving, and repentance that will radically change us by reforming our lives. These resolutions do not have to be like the New Year's ones, generally thought of in negative terms of giving up something. Rather these practices should be looked at positively as gifts, as behaviors that will energize us and bring us closer to God and each other. Our failures can limit or challenge us, the holidays can be happy or sad, the winter cold or warm, we can look forward or backward. Being with John shows us the way.

Today is *Gaudete* Sunday, the Sunday of rejoicing in Advent, for Christmas and all that it signifies is almost here. What progress have we made, like John, in understanding the importance of this preparatory period? Have we prayed, given alms, and repented through action over words? Have we given locally and globally, prayed privately and in community? It will be Christmas soon in Africa, India, and the United States. In contemporary life, will all recognize the significance of the Incarnation? The fulfillment of the promise of God the father in Genesis to send his son is at hand. The pink candle has been lit. What does that mean to you?

THE FOURTH SUNDAY IN ADVENT: BEHOLD, THE LAMB OF GOD (JOHN 1:36)

Even the animals and the stars, and the lowly shepherds recognized God at his birth. The intelligence of living matter knows its creator. Advent has been the training period to know God in a new way at Christmas, and hopefully our brief journey with John helped us to share the clarity of one man who was not superfluous, who only realized God was coming into the world to save us, and nothing was more important than getting ready for that by giving up sin.

John didn't have an Advent wreath to mark off the time preparing for the Lord, and it was more than four weeks that he waited. We have now lit the Advent wreath weekly, sent the Christmas cards, and bought most of the presents. People have been invited to dinner and the tree is up and decorated. We will no doubt have a rich Christmas—lots of food, presents and precious time with loved ones. We will feel warmth, comfort, and full. The house will be clean and decorated and our tummies more than satisfied, but millions will never experience Christmas the way we do or the way John did as he ate insects and wild honey in the desert. Is it as simple as cleanliness being next to godliness? Do we feel like leaping as John did into another reality, the reality of the spirit, the reality of limitless, loving service?

The nativity of St. John the Baptist on June 24 is the oldest church feast. Now, six months later, it is the nativity of Jesus. The only other nativity that we celebrate as a church is the nativity of Mary his mother. The point is, John is important, and yet he is mysterious, a man of few words and an intensity we may think fanatical, but really he understood the signs of the times and the nature of reality and was not as countercultural as we may think. We have had a chance to spend a brief time trying to understand what he did—that nothing is more important than God in our lives.

The early church understood John but we still come to Mass failing to be loving to those around us, avoiding to practice inclusivity, ignoring the poor or those who don't believe or who are not like us even in our own families. Many churches and locations claim to have John's head. Imagine the beautiful head of St. John the Baptist! It is a popular painting. In later centuries some even put his head on a cake platter to make that incident relevant to the people. It would be incredible to see it and yet John would tell us that where his head is does not matter, only where our head is and it belongs to God.

John is unfathomable, admirable, and inimitable; wild, wooly, and radically practical, a passionate preacher pointing to Jesus, our Savior. Yet he is all of the things we are—patient and impatient, empty and full, suffering from heat and cold, repenting and rejoicing. We deserve no more than camel's hair, and yet it would be enough for life does have another dimension. So come Lord Jesus this Christmas to us in a new way. We await all the cultural comforts and spiritual joys of Christmas, and hasten to share them because they are but a foretaste of heaven, and we are not afraid anymore to lose our heads over you. As God the father proclaimed at Jesus' Baptism and at the transfiguration, for Christmas, and for all time, "This is my beloved Son, with whom I am well pleased" (Matt 3:17).

3

Special Supplement for Advent and Christmas II

The Word of God in the Old Testament for Advent—Christ, the New Creation

Christmas candle wreath flowers

INTRODUCTION: THE WORD OF GOD IN THE OLD TESTAMENT FOR ADVENT—CHRIST, THE NEW CREATION

At the end of the calendar year and the beginning of the church's liturgical year, we make room in our hearts and community to welcome the savior into the world at Christmas. In order to assist us in the transition towards this momentous event, it is an "adventitious" time when we can reacquaint ourselves with the sacred history of the human race found in the richness of story and the word of God in the Old Testament. In this short, weekly series, the fundamental theme of the Old Testament—the fidelity of God the father for his fallen creation that includes both humankind and nature, and the plan for their release from bondage—emerges. Maybe during Advent we can gain a glimpse of his great love for his children and come to appreciate the impenetrable sacrifice of obedience found in his son Jesus Christ and the love of the spirit who come to repair our estranged friendships.

The Old Testament is sacred history—the firm Jewish and Christian belief that God acts in human history, and that God's saving acts are central in the lives and history of the people of the Jewish Scripture, complemented with humanity's response to him. It reminds us that God is not only revealed to us, but lovingly acts and interacts with us, still in our day, our community, our parish, and in the context of our own human and individual experience.

Careful study of the Old Testament texts and the way they were written has shown us that it is generally not their purpose to present history in the factual or literal sense. These are sacred texts meant to reveal the religious truth about God through the "meaning" of whatever events are recounted, first and foremost for the Hebrews. It is our modern day challenge as well as for all time for us as Catholics to learn how to read the Old Testament as sacred history. It is a hard, laborious but joyful task to become acquainted with the word of God in the Old Testament. Under the guidance of the Holy Spirit, the soul of the church, we come to cherish the holy story that is our own.

Advent is a new beginning and a good time to deepen our appreciation of the mystery and reality of the Incarnation that we experience again in the new liturgical year wherein we will follow the radical message of discipleship found in the first Gospel, the Gospel of Mark, read in Year B of the church calendar. St. Jerome, considered the greatest Doctor of the Catholic Church for his knowledge of the Bible, tells us that every

very single page of either testament seems to center around Christ. One stream flows out from the throne of God, and that is the grace of the Holy Spirit, and that grace of the Holy Spirit is in the Holy Scriptures. Yet that stream has twin banks, the Old Testament and the New, and the tree planted on either side is Christ. This Advent, this special season of joyful anticipation, let us envision that the tree Jerome speaks about, the tree of testaments, will come to us as our greatest gift beneath the Christmas tree as we answer in our individual way, by virtue of our call through Baptism, the question—who is this child born unto us?

THE FIRST WEEK OF ADVENT:
THE BOOK OF GENESIS 1–3

All of us know something about the Book of Genesis. We probably think of it as the first book in the Old Testament and that is certainly true in terms of its literary placement in the drama of story construction. Interestingly, Genesis, a most poetic account of the creation of the world, was one of the last books of the Old Testament, written during the Babylonian exile of the Hebrews from 597 to 581 BCE. During this period, the well-known oral traditions and foundational memories of the Hebrews were recorded in remembrance of the active, historical role of God in their lives, as well as to help them distinguish themselves from their captors, and to aid in forging a unique Jewish identity so vital to life in captivity. The Jews, like most peoples, needed a creation story to answer the basic questions that all of us grapple with individually and as a society. Who are we? Where did we come from? Where are we going? What is our relationship to God? These were the questions that demanded the answers recorded in Genesis.

Genesis is an artistic and insightful blend of two creation accounts constructed by two different groups of biblical writers in the Priestly and the Yahwist traditions. The Priestly account emphasized the majestic transcendence of God, while the Yahwist writers saw the divine closely connected to humanity. Together they offer us a balanced and rich concept of God as both transcendent and immanent. In Genesis, God brings order to chaos, and through his imagination, love, and creativity, makes the world and sets in motion the laws of the universe. Light and dark, the dome of sky and ocean, seed-bearing trees, birds of the air, fish of the sea, and all kinds of creeping things are created. Each has its place in the order of life. The final creation, humankind, is put at the head of caring for the world. Dominion was not meant to be an act of domination, but in line with the stewardship, love, and care the creator had for all his creation that we are invited to share.

But as we know it didn't take long for the harmony of life in the garden to become disrupted, and the fall ensued. Some say it involved a serpent and an apple, but we know today from the aid of the historical-critical method of investigation into the times that the literary genre was constructed, that the alienation that ensued between humankind and God, the original sin, was one of disobedience. We love or we don't, and that love translates into obedience and free choice in gratitude for the gift of life. So expulsion from the accessible company of God came about. God in his infinite goodness wanted us as companions, and so a solution had to be achieved. Even with the fall God remained faithful to his rebellious creation and Genesis tells the story of God's faithfulness to his disobedient but loved children, and his gracious attempt to restore right relationships between himself and humanity. A reconciler who could only be God would come who would mend the brokenness of the world. The rest of the story is about humanity and God's tortuous yet loving reconciliation with each together over time, culminating in his son Jesus, the continuum of the new creation, born at Christmas.

In the Advent season, Genesis is relevant in many ways. It encapsulates an explanation for a world of imperfection, pain, suffering, death, and toil, a world we know so well. We are left poised at odds with nature, the world we were meant to live in harmony with, but one that was cursed and remains so today through our neglect of responsibility towards the planet. Advent is a pregnant season of new beginnings for relationships and the way we live in the world. It is an open window that lets in the light of joyful anticipation and hope that frees us from our alienation. Christ, the New Creation, comes this Advent. Can you see him approaching in a winter star, an opalescent sky holding a pearl of great price? He is in the verdant Advent wreath, the early morning cloak of snow where the world is reborn again in peace, reconciliation, and new life. Genesis is a story of love and fidelity. Advent is the same story.

THE SECOND WEEK OF ADVENT: ABRAHAM AND ELECTION IN GENESIS

In the sacred history of the inspired Old Testament texts, we find stories we remember more than others due to their drama or significance.

One such account is the narrative of God establishing a very special and intimate relationship with Abraham. In Genesis, their relationship is depicted as so natural—God talks and Abraham responds—revealing how close Abraham was to God, and how much God favored Abraham with his presence and his promises. Abraham, despite his flaws and struggles, was available and accessible to a will and a plan other than his own. He is deemed a father of a chosen nation, beloved of God, ultimately for his obedience. The stories of Abraham and his wife Sarah are full of hope, trust, and love of God, with some moments of incredulity and duplicity, not unlike our own relationship with God.

In Genesis 12 God called Abram to set out for the land of Canaan with his wife and Lot, his brother's son. When Abram reached the land it was experiencing famine, and so he traveled on to Egypt. Prior to his travels God promised to make of Abram a great nation. He was blessed by God, told his name would be great, and all would be blessed who bless him and cursed if they cursed him. All the communities of the earth would find blessing in him. This is a tremendous declaration by God, conferring the fatherhood of nations to Abram, and establishing a covenantal, never to be broken relationship between God and his chosen people.

In Genesis 15 the word of God came in a vision to Abram, again promising him great rewards and a land to possess. But without a son Abram felt these gifts had no meaning. The Lord promised Abram he would have a son and that his heirs would be as numerous as the stars. Abram believed this promise and he offered a sacrifice to God thereby sealing the covenant. God continued to promise Abram in Genesis 17 that he would be the father of nations, the land of Canaan would be his, and God would be the God of his people. Abram's name was changed to Abraham. God asked as part of this covenant that all males be circumcised and God declared, "Thus my covenant shall be in your flesh as an everlasting pact" (Gen 17:13). Sarai's name was changed to Sarah, and God promised that Sarah in her old age would conceive a son to be named Isaac. The promise of a son was fulfilled as part of this new nation, foreshadowing the coming of God's own son, who unlike Isaac, would not be spared but must be given over as part of a new covenant.

God elected his people, Israel, and through Abraham and his descendants, God vowed to be with them and us for all time despite our imperfections. Through our patriarch Abraham's devotion and faithfulness, and even his indiscretions, we learn to trust in God's enduring presence and what it means to be a person of faith. The plan of God is now revealed as a universal one—"All the communities of the earth shall find blessing in you" "(Gen 12:3). We are part of that plan, brought back to the fullness of life, dreamed for all time by a faithful God.

Sacrifice, sorrow, mystery, and miracles are part of the experience that accompanied the birth of a nation. Advent has its promises, miracles and sorrows too. Can we in this season have the hopeful trust of Abraham to the point of sacrificing everything? Can we start our church year with the unwavering trust of Abraham in God despite financial problems, unemployment, a depressed economy, or illness, old age, and the stresses of life? Can we see Jesus enfleshed in the starving faces of African children and those hungry for his word and do something about it? What can you do this week, in imitation of the hopeful trust and anticipation of Abraham and Sarah and the coming of Jesus? The family has begun with Abraham as the father of nations, and today we are his children, grafted to the olive tree that is Israel, through Jesus. We are the grain of sand, a twinkling star, and a holy people told in Genesis, who faithfully and patiently await his son this Advent.

THE THIRD WEEK OF ADVENT AND *GAUDETE* SUNDAY: THE BOOK OF EXODUS

No study of the Old Testament would be complete without considering the central role of Moses in sacred history. Moses of lowly origins, like that of Jesus, is found in a basket in the Nile and raised a pharaoh's son. As Moses grew into awareness of who he was, slave and Hebrew, he was mandated to free God's chosen people and lead them to their own land, never to enter it himself, for his failure like ours, to trust that God is faithful.

Exodus is the second book of the Old Testament and one of the five books of the Pentateuch, the record of the religious history of the Israelite people, their liberation from Egypt, and their birth as a nation. The date for the actual exodus is most likely between 1300 and 1280 BCE. Like Genesis, the book of Exodus was constructed during the Babylonian exile much later in the sixth through fifth centuries BCE, a time when the oral traditions and culture of the Israelites and their encounter with God was recorded. In Exodus, Moses takes the people on one of the greatest journeys ever known, from Egyptian slavery, to the land flowing with milk and honey. Along the way, in the figurative forty years in the desert, God supplies his people with *manna*, a mysterious food that came down from heaven. There are strict orders on how much *manna* to gather and when, such as a double portion for the Sabbath, but not all listen. For some, the mystery of the *manna* might be stripped away if our understanding of it narrows to a natural occurrence, like nectar gathered from an insect, or dew that precipitated in the desert, but nevertheless, through the divine working in nature, it was delicious, nutritious, and supplied by God.

Today many focus on the interpretation of the *manna* as our figurative daily bread, and the foreshadowing of the Eucharist as the food of life (Rev 2:17). While the analogy of *manna* can be compared and contrasted to the eucharistic body of Christ to come through the Incarnation, the *manna* story, as an Old Testament account, was first a lesson for the Israelites. The central theme woven throughout the Old Testament, on the tests of obedience that God required of his people in order to bring them to a fuller life of freedom, was learned. Bonded by trust in God's fidelity, the Israelites learned God was with them always and would feed them. What an astounding thought! The *manna* was his food; the *manna* was his word!

Thematically, this tale of wilderness wanderings is an exile story. Four familiar themes of Exodus in the *manna* story surface: a problem arises, the people complain, Moses as an intimate friend with God intercedes for his people, and God delivers them. The economic model of Egypt was one of slavery and scarcity, but the deliverance from Egypt by God was an act of freedom and abundance.

Abundance, in Hebrew, *dayenu*, is not a material state but a mental one. Advent is a time of *dayenu*, the abundant love of God for his people through the birth of his son and what is to come. This week, can we make a habit of practicing discipleship with the *dayenu* of the Sinai in the desert of our lives? When Christ came he said he came to give us life and to have it more abundantly. He is not talking about Christmas presents, food, money, and the luxuries of the season, but the bread of his life as food. By relying on the generosity of God, can we free ourselves from legitimate monetary worries to focus on the *manna* as the word of God? Poised within our pluralistic community where the poor are less visible, the homeless and hungry hidden, prisoners concealed, the ill homebound or hospitalized, can we as a parish and individually surpass our normal generosity of giving with money, food, goods and service, in a radical transformation of love that is Jesus, not just in Advent but also as a lifestyle of *dayenu*?

Advent is a hopeful exodus. Our enslavement is broken by his enfleshment. Life is abundant in the desert wilderness. There is enough, there has always been enough. From the *manna*, to the multiplication of the loaves, to the institution of the Eucharist, the sacrament of his flesh is given. God not only lives among his people but in them. He took on flesh and has never left us. This is the story of Exodus and Advent.

THE FOURTH WEEK OF ADVENT: PROPHETS AND THE BOOK OF KINGS

Many but not all cultures have had a monarchy period. About 1200 to 1050 BCE, the Israelites desired a king, and envisioned their land as a place where a powerful king like those of other nations would reign. But as the Deuteronomistic historians tell us, overall the monarchy was not the most glorious time in Israel's history. Was the monarchy doomed from the beginning as a political style, or was its failure the function of the leaders? Were the monarchs like Saul, Solomon, and the popular David as imperfect by human governmental standards as the sacred history writers portrayed them? Was it because they failed to model their leadership style on the king of their nation begun by Abraham and bequeathed to David and his family for all time? This was a king they should have known by his kingly qualities, the one they knew best, because he was ever faithful to them in times of suffering and abundance. The practicality of politics and the seduction of power got in the way of Israel's fidelity to the king who had been with them on their journeys from Egypt to the Promised Land. Their true king was like no other—magnanimous in mercy, unerring in forgiveness, steadfast in slavery, and beneficent in promises. He was Yahweh in their midst, his glory manifest in the Ark of the Covenant, and the verdant Promised Land.

The covenantal relationship continued between God and his people through David, with many interrelated promises from God that the house of Israel would be blessed forever. In 2 Samuel 7 God promised David through Nathan that David would be famous, God would plant Israel on land, the wicked would not afflict the Israelites, God would give them rest and establish a house for the Israelites, and God would raise up an heir and make David's kingdom firm even if he did wrong. David's house and kingdom would endure forever. This is a further election narrative within the sacred history of Israel. Look at what God offers Israel through David and see how beautifully David responds and glorifies God. It is an unconditional covenant. David does not have to do anything, but God would like a temple to be built. This seems to be a device in which God seems to say, "I have no temple, just like you have had no home, but still I am willing to give you all this. Trust in me."

While both the Mosaic and Davidic covenants are initiated by God, and are different, they are interrelated. God's covenants build upon the subsequent ones and culminate with the new covenant achieved by Jesus' death. The basis of the covenant with David is foundational. It assumes that commandments are the infrastructure of the social order such that God can offer his posterity all these things. It is an augmentation of God's fidelity and love of his chosen people who will eventually, through the house of David, bring us the Messiah at Christmas.

In the texts of Kings and Amos we see how history was rewritten by the Deuteronomistic historians to show the lessons learned that constitute sacred history. Solomon was a materialistic king and a tyrant. While he did not go to war, he modeled himself after other traditional monarchies that were not consonant with the Israelite's identification as a chosen people. His reign was reminiscent of slavery in Egypt. They did not portray him in a good light because they wanted to contrast him to his father, the beloved King David. Characteristic of many failed governments to the present time, Solomon did not understand the common people, never mind the poor, and his failure to perceive such social realities did not endear him to his people. We remember Solomon in the Old Testament for his wisdom over the child who was claimed by two mothers almost exclusively presented from the perspective of his wisdom, without the implication that he might have actually split the child in half because he was a tyrannical king! Still, if God asked us, would we respond with a pure heart as Solomon did? Could we give up our most precious things to give life to others? This is what he is asking us this Advent. Who is the king? What is a king? How does a king act? What is our kingly role in the here and coming kingdom of God?

CHRISTMAS—O WONDROUS FIDELITY!
CHRIST, THE NEW CREATION

The bare aspen tree, as naked as the newborn child, has been replaced with the fullness of creation by the stately, fragrant, Christmas tree, green with life. Both hover near the altar. They know their place; they know their nature. The God of the New Testament—he is love and mercy. All of our thoughts and deeds are measured by this standard. The God of the Old Testament, the one who seemed to largely appear in gathering clouds or a burning bush, had special relationships with extraordinary servants like Moses, Abraham and David. This is what so many encounters were about in the books of the Old Testament—covenants of love with chosen people and creation, and unfailing fidelity—a comforting theme as we struggle with the Israelites in Egypt, the wilderness, the exile, and the postexilic period, and back to remembrance of the garden. Fidelity means everything! It frees us from the illusion of control, and allows us to experience our daily bread. The struggle through the Old Testament is a lot of work, but look what we have learned—a God who exceeds definition, a God of abundance, delight, love, mercy, and most of all fidelity! His fidelity is as certain as the sun and the stars, and now so in Christ, the new creation. His constancy means we must reciprocate and be faithful as well in our relationships with family, friends, community, the parish, and the world, and in the ministry of the church in a "new" Old Testament way. As Advent ends, hopefully we have had new encounters with and within the church, nature, and ourselves and the world. The list is unlimited.

Some scholars maintain that the baby alluded to in the beautiful poetic prophecy of Isaiah 9 is future King Hezekiah. It seems this is true in light of much sacred history, which had significance that pertained to the audience living at that time. However, another cardinal characteristic of sacred history is that it is the living word of God, and as such it is a chronicle that becomes re-read and reinterpreted in latter history by biblical authors, sometimes all the way through the New Testament in what is called *sensus plenior,* or the fuller sense not evident at the time of the prophet.

The latter Jews of Jesus' time, upon hearing this divine scenario of Isaiah, might have believed the monarchy would once more be restored to Israel, and an earthly kingdom with glory established with an ideal king similar to David or even Hezekiah at the helm. This would be supported in their view as fulfillment of the covenant that God made with David that a firm throne would be established, and their belief that God would never abandon them. A new kingdom with a king sent directly by Yahweh would create a golden age, and in Isaiah's authoritative language as a messenger of God, it seemed inevitable. This world of Isaiah 9 could come about if the Jews took Yahweh seriously. Social justice would be attained. This is a common thematic structure of Isaiah where the Lord appears, he invites a response from his people, and he intervenes to save them. Today, Christmas, Jesus is his new invitation and his intervention. What is our response?

Isaiah need not have known the full force latent in his own words of the child born of a virgin. Christians would later reinterpret the sacred texts that are our roots and apply these prophecies to Jesus born of the Virgin Mary. But as we know the Holy Spirit was preparing for a nativity of one greater than any who had come before through his birth with the Virgin Mary. Advent has been fulfilled. Do we understand the word of God any better? St. Jerome said Jesus is the tree that links the Old and the New Testament. We meet him today in the Christmas tree, and "the leaves of the tree are for the healing of the nations" (Rev 22:2).

4

The Christmas Season and Pre-Lent Ordinary Time

AN OVERVIEW

ORDINARY TIME COMPRISES THE majority of the weeks of the liturgical and calendar year consisting of thirty-three to thirty-four weeks depending on the liturgical year. It is divided into two parts. Because the start of the liturgical year varies each year, as well as the start of Lent, there is a short period of the four to nine weeks between the Christmas season and Lent, which is part of Ordinary Time. After Easter and its post-Easter season, following Pentecost, Ordinary Time resumes again until the Feast of Christ the King. Ordinary Time is the period that is not exclusively dedicated to the anticipation of Jesus in Advent and at Christmas, or his death and resurrection in Lent and at Easter.

To derive the greatest value from this book, instead of limiting it to one liturgical year, since they are never the same, I have separated the readings under those that clearly can be used for Advent and Christmas, and Lent and Easter, and the fifty-day Easter season. All others are referenced by the fixed feast or if clearly under Ordinary Time. The reader should consult the Contents for the liturgical period or feast for the week or topic of interest.

THE FEAST OF THE HOLY FAMILY: BY THE POWER OF THE HOLY SPIRIT HE WAS BORN OF THE VIRGIN MARY, AND BECAME MAN

The first Sunday after Christmas we celebrate the Feast of the Holy Family. Seasonally, it is likewise a good day to rejoice as many people are still traveling and visiting relatives as part of the Christmas season. It is a precious time to spend together in the company of loved ones at Mass and at home.

Jesus, Mary, and Joseph are the Holy Family. At first glance, because they are so saintly, we may not know how to relate to them or think they are not relevant to our lives. But they were human too. They had worry, heartache, confusion, fear, loneliness, poverty; all the things we too experience. What made them holy was the way they accepted their experiences with a faith so embedded in their lives that they could accept the bewildering things presented to them—apparitions by angels, the virgin birth, the flight to Egypt, and death on a cross. This unassuming pure girl and the hard working obedient man, through their acquiescence, became the parents of Jesus, and the mother and father of the church.

In an era of unprecedented divorce and change in the family structure, the Holy Family has great meaning for us. Our fractured, suffering families, torn by war, financial difficulties, chronic degenerative illness, poverty, and the unparalleled stress of modern day life need a model for practical and spiritual living. At a time when technologically and globally the human family has never been closer, we are in many ways the most distant we have ever been. We need to call on the Holy Family by modeling their humility and obedience to God. At all costs they were here to protect life and to reclaim it for God. It is our calling too.

Despite the cultural changes that are part and parcel of any era, we can always feel love and bestow it as they did through the divine nature of our humanity. We were born in his image and likeness, born into a human family, and baptized into the family of the church. The same things that unite us can divide us unless they are overcome with love. Through the love of Christ and the intercession the Holy Family we can create a holy family for the world and ourselves.

THE FEAST OF THE HOLY FAMILY: HONOR THY FATHER AND THY MOTHER (ALTERNATIVE VERSION)

All families are meant to be holy. Modeled after the simplicity and humility of Jesus, Mary, and Joseph, we were created to be a nuclear family, the smallest and most important of our social institutions, a structure that supports our growth and development, protecting, nurturing, caring, and loving us from natural conception to natural death. All of our other social institutions—educational, political, financial and religious—are as good as this foundation. Is it any wonder today that the health of the planet and the social order is so precarious when they are built upon families that are incomplete, fragmented, and wounded, made so by war, violence, illness, and choice?

The preponderance of the world has family problems. Some of us have wonderful family lives that perpetuate family values and structure. The family is a strength and a refuge. To create such a family is not without challenges and difficulties, but to do so is a natural extension of love, which when understood and coupled with faith, can sustain us. Other families suffer separation, persecutions, poverty, illness and broken hearts. But even broken bones become stronger when they heal, and we are more than bones. We are family.

We worry about the future, wonder why things are the way they are, accept mystery and suffering, gladness and goodness, and still push forward with trust in the Lord. We can look to Jesus, Mary, and Joseph, a very small family unit but the example of how we should be. The flight to Egypt was not exotic, but the point is, a trusting family undertook it.

Each generation aspires to more for our families. It is natural to want to give them more than we had, and the gifts of comfort are good when we can share them and they don't get in the way of our relationship with God, family, or humanity. We can be like the Holy Family, whose life was not self-serving, who humbly accepted simplicity and poverty, and the visit of lowly shepherds along with that of great learned kings. The reality of the downward mobility of the Incarnation makes it possible for us to believe that despite our station in life nothing is more important than receiving God into our lives through family as the greatest gift we can receive.

To a certain extent it is true that we enter into the world and leave it alone, but it is equally as true that we enter and leave in the context of some semblance of family and they are all that is in-between. The adage that blood is thicker than water implies that the ties that bind between relatives are stronger than those who are not related to us. But the commingling of blood and water from the side of Christ crucified is the intermediary that unites us all in the family of God. We are the "us" in Jesus. This Sunday, the last Sunday of the calendar year, is the Feast of the Holy Family. It is our feast. Let us end it and begin it with family.

THE NEW YEAR: THE ONE WHO DOES JUSTICE WILL LIVE IN THE PRESENCE OF THE LORD*

January is a month of new beginnings. This month several notable events are observed—the week for Prayer for Christian Unity, Martin Luther King Day, the Pro-life Mass, and the state of the union address. They are things to look back and reflect upon, and to look forward to with new understandings. Ultimately they can be days of hope that can promote inclusion and the celebration of the gift of Christ with our fellow Christians, the dream of equal rights for African Americans conceived so long ago and now achieved through the election of a President, for penance for millions of unborn Americans who our culture failed by confusing legality with morality, and the celebration of the gift of life in all its stages, and for our mutual union as American people.

The ecumenical movement has done many things to bring us closer as a Christian community, largely through the willingness of church leaders to listen to each other, along with the power of shared prayer and services. The impossible dream of a black political preacher became a reality with the election of a black President in 2008 that changed history forever. While the incalculable devastation of life from Roe vs. Wade can never be undone, its perpetuation is not inevitable nor is its interpretation. The pro-life issue is a primary topic in the presidential elections, and regardless of their verbal position on the issue, it is a subject important enough to be courageously articulated on the nightly news. Social change begins with recognition, articulation, and dialogue on issues, so there is hope that with conversation, conversion, and prayer that the most helpless of our society from the unborn to the elderly will be acknowledged with their God-given dignity.

The New Year began with the Solemnity of Mary, and on that day we heard Simeon disclose to Mary the first of her seven sorrows—that her son would be opposed. She learned this just eight days after his birth on the day he was brought to the temple to be named! Three of Mary's seven sorrows occur when Jesus is a child—the prophecy of Simeon, the flight to Egypt, and his loss in the temple for three days. The other four center around the passion—Mary meeting him at Calvary, standing at the foot of the cross as he dies, her presence as Jesus is taken down from the cross, and the burial of Jesus. Surely as a mother Mary endured more than seven sorrows, but these seven are the inordinate sufferings of the Mother of God. For us they are ways of framing and organizing experience into some sense and meditations like the mysteries of the rosary or the Stations of the Cross. These sorrows unfold liturgically and we can use them to reflect upon in connection with the sorrow of religious separation, residual racism, the scourge of abortion, and lack of respect for life at all stages, and political imperfection.

Let us invoke our mother Mary, Mother of God, who is the patroness of the Americas, for guidance. Let us remember her immeasurable sorrow in light of the ones we share, but also her faith and trust in God that life can spring from suffering. Every New Year is a year pregnant with hope if we unite ourselves to Mary's unconditional love and example for the sacredness of human life. It can be a happy new year in America, one it seems we have always been waiting for in the political, social, economic, ecclesiastical and moral arenas—the renewal of the dignity of all life, and the hope in the future, both incalculable gifts from our loving God.

*Responsorial Psalm

THE FEAST OF THE SOLEMNITY OF THE BLESSED VIRGIN MARY AND THE FEAST OF THE EPIPHANY: THE MIGHTY ONE HAS DONE GREAT THINGS FOR ME AND HOLY IS HIS NAME (ALTERNATIVE VERSION) (LUKE 1:49)

January 1, the octave of Christmas, is the first day of the New Year, the first holyday of obligation of the year in most countries, and a holiday. It is the Feast of the Solemnity of the Blessed Virgin Mary, a feast that the honors the privilege of Mary as Mother of God. Prior to 1960 this day was called the Circumcision of Jesus, denoting the fulfillment of the Jewish expectation of circumcision of males eight days after birth as a sign of the covenant between God and Abraham. It was an act attesting to the human nature of Jesus and his willingness to fulfill the law. On this day the child was also officially named, and Jesus, meaning "savior" received his name from God. Culturally, is a day of celebration—football games, special food, New Year's resolutions expressing our desire for a clean slate to start over, and the official end of the holiday season. But it is the real beginning of a new covenant when physical circumcision is no longer needed, but the new requirement for all to throw off the burden of sin. The four dogmas about Mary—her Immaculate Conception, her perpetual virginity, and her Assumption into heaven are a consequence of this primary role as the Mother of God celebrated this day.

Later this week we celebrate the Feast of the Epiphany, the official end of the church's Christmas season. Then Ordinary Time will briefly resume before Lent. We know the feast of the Epiphany as the day that the three kings arrived from the East, following the cosmic event of a special star that was prophetic of the birth of a new king. Legend says they were three, some say as many as twelve, that they were of different races, some even say this is a mythological way of expressing the adoration of the Savior by the human race.

In Cologne, Germany, at the Cologne Cathedral dedicated to St. Peter and the Blessed Virgin Mary, there is a world famous shrine housing several Catholic treasures, foremost of which is the Shrine of the Three Kings. The Archbishop of Cologne acquired their relics in 1164, when the Holy Roman Emperor, Frederick Barbarossa took them from Milan, Italy. Their bones and 2000-year-old clothes rest in the largest reliquary in the western world, a large gold sarcophagus. It is believed they were martyred when they returned to their lands bringing the news of the newborn king who was God. Another of its treasures is its twelve bells with the Bell of the Three Kings weighing almost four tons. A star instead of a cross crowns the spire of the church. It seems our persistent recognition of the Magi is not unfounded.

So the Christmas trees will come down, the New Year's resolutions will be made and inevitably broken, but the gift Mary and her willingness to be our intercessor, and the adoration by three kings of an infant in a stable, remind us of the willingness of God to come to the human race. Our heritage, education, gender, wealth, age, ethnicity, and status are made insignificant in the presence of the eternal God who through love became man in a child so we could become a child of God.

> *A solemnity is a principal holy day commemorating an event in the life of Jesus, Mary, or the saints.

THE MOST HOLY NAME OF JESUS AND THE FEAST OF THE EPIPHANY: O COME LET US ADORE HIM (ALTERNATIVE VERSION)

The three magi traveled far and wide led by the star in the belief that the Savior of the world had come amongst us. Yet even though he ascended into heaven two thousand years ago, he has dwelt with us, whole and entire, visibly in our churches, in the most Blessed Sacrament. He is here as he said he would be until the end of time, fully human and divine, as real as the child in the manger or the lamb with the cross.

One of the things which makes us uniquely Catholic is our belief in his real and actual presence under the species of the consecrated host which we have the privilege of receiving in Holy Communion, and viewing and adoring during the Exposition of the Most Blessed Sacrament on special feast days and the First Friday of each month. Many saints and writers such as St. Thomas More, St. Francis Xavier, and St. John Vianney have recounted their mystical, almost indescribable experiences and blessings received during Eucharistic Adoration. Wonderful books such as *Visits to the Blessed Sacrament and Our Lady* by St. Alphonsus Liguori remind us of the sanctifying graces given to us for our weak condition and sinful world when we give praise and thanks and even implore our incarnate Lord for his life-giving grace. Even unbelievers knowingly gasp in awe, and been moved by viewing the sacred body enthroned in the gold monstrance, not quite capturing its significance, but observably changed and altered by it.

The practice of First Friday adoration was revealed to St. Margaret Mary Alacoque as something Jesus desired for our benefit. By faithfully devoting oneself to this practice for nine consecutive months, not only do we have the humbling yet exalted privilege of being in our divine Lord's presence, but also we can reap unique graces, so great is his love for us. He promises to those who observe First Friday:

1. I will give to my faithful all the graces necessary in their state of life.
2. I will establish peace in their homes.
3. I will comfort them in all their afflictions.
4. I will be their secure refuge during life, and above all in death.
5. I will bestow abundant blessings upon on all their undertakings.
6. Sinners shall find in my heart the source and the infinite ocean of mercy.
7. Tepid souls shall become fervent.
8. Fervent souls shall quickly mount to high perfection.
9. I will bless every place in which an image of my heart shall be exposed and honored.

10. I will give to priests the gift of touching the most hardened hearts.

11. Those who shall promote this devotion shall have their names written in my heart never to be effaced.

12. I promise you in the excessive mercy of my heart, that my all-powerful love will grant to all those who communicate on the First Friday in nine consecutive months the grace of final penitence; they shall not die in my disgrace, nor without receiving their sacraments. My divine heart shall be their safe refuge in this last moment.

How could we not want these gifts? On the Feast of the Epiphany, in this New Year, let us make a promise, like Jesus that we will not break, a personal pledge to come and adore him as often as we can in monthly First Friday Adoration. O come Let us adore him.

THE FEAST OF THE BAPTISM OF THE LORD: GO THEREFORE AND MAKE FOLLOWERS OF ALL NATIONS, BAPTIZING THEM IN THE NAME OF THE FATHER, AND OF THE SON AND OF THE HOLY SPIRIT (MATT 28:19)

This week we celebrate the Feast of the Baptism of the Lord by St. John the Baptist, an event that marks the beginning of Jesus' public life. It is the conclusion of the weeks of preparation and celebration of Christmas and its many sacred mysteries. Baptism, meaning "the plunge," is the beginning of our life in Christ when we can share in the divine through Baptism just as Jesus, the divine, became human with the Incarnation.

Whether as infants, children, or adult catechumens, our initiation into the church, the spiritual richness of the sacraments, and our eternal life with God, is initiated through the waters of Baptism that symbolize the fluid grace it confers. Even Jesus was baptized showing us that the way to the father is through the spirit. The sanctifying grace of the Holy Spirit marks us indelibly with the sign of faith, a seal which will influence our lives, especially if we help keep it alive through membership in the church by renewing our baptismal vows today, when we say the Creed at Mass, or at the beginning of the rosary, and when we witness baptisms throughout the year, at the Easter vigil, and during the Easter season.

Following this feast, Ordinary Time is launched for a short period, each year dependent upon the liturgical calendar. Lent begins on Ash Wednesday. As a church, during Lent, Baptism becomes a major focus leading to Easter. Soon we also celebrate more than one hundred years of the Week of Prayer for Christian Unity. This octave is devoted to the effort to work toward understanding and reconciliation of various Christian traditions. While differences exist between them such as the issues of the importance of Mary, the real presence of God in the Eucharist, the infallibility of the pope on matters of faith, contraception, and other matters, one thing we all have in common is belief in Baptism. There is only one Baptism and one spirit.

So the Christmas season is over until next year, but our new life can begin because Jesus came into the world and showed us the way home through the blessed waters of Baptism when we become a child of God.

THE FEAST OF THE BAPTISM OF THE LORD: CONSUBSTANTIAL WITH THE FATHER (ALTERNATIVE VERSION)

Just as life emerged from the waters of creation and the fluid world of the womb, our life in Christ begins with Baptism The first decade of the Luminous Mysteries of the rosary is the Baptism of Jesus. This is such a beautiful image. Jesus, humbled and stripped, is standing in the calm Jordan River as it slowly meanders through the verdant Jordan Valley. John the Baptist, who leapt in his mother's womb when Mary and Elizabeth greeted each other in their pregnancies, now baptizes Jesus. How does he feel ministering to his cousin, the son of God, whom he has been preaching about? Would we like John know the God we proclaim to love when he is right in front of us in every single person?

As the clouds part and the sun shines on Jesus, the father's voice deeply emerges from the mideastern sky, "This is my beloved Son in whom I am well pleased." Despite our disappointments and expectations can we say that to each other, to our friends, our children, our students, and our parents instead of calling them losers or failures? It feels good to be appreciated. Even God told his son that.

Epidemiology, the study of infectious disease patterns, claims in new research, that mental states such as happiness are a lot like the transmission of an illness. Simply summarized, if we are happy, we can spread it even if we don't know the other people! Relationship is more powerful than environment in shaping the world. We can share our happiness over the Good News through our network of all we meet.

Baptism confers an imprint that will shape the rest of our lives, consciously or not. Some Christian traditions think one should choose Christ as an adult before being baptized but that is what Confirmation currently is in the Catholic tradition. Cultural exposure to television, family, peers, and school begins immediately after birth, as should our life in God through Baptism. We can never come close enough to God. Infants should be baptized as soon as possible to give them this spiritual DNA of sorts to help us grow as children of God. This is also *National Vocations Awareness Week*. Jesus' public life began with Baptism. In these difficult times job security may be tenuous, but to do God's will is our true vocation, not our employment or our marital status. This vocation starts with Baptism.

THE FEASTS OF ST. PAUL, ST. THOMAS AQUINAS AND ST. FRANCIS DE SALES: WE ARE WRITING YOU THIS SO THAT OUR JOY WILL BE COMPLETE (1 JOHN 1:4)

JANUARY 25, 28 AND 29 RESPECTIVELY

St. Thomas Aquinas—we've all heard his name before, but even if we don't remember much about him we know that if saints have stature he is surely one of them. Born into a noble family in the thirteenth century in Naples, Italy, he entered the Dominican order as foretold to his mother by a holy hermit who claimed, "So great will be his learning and sanctity that in his day no one will be found equal to him." At a young age he was "girdled with chastity" by an angel, an event that allowed the purity of his spirit to overflow into his prolific and prestigious writings, and yet he always cloaked himself in humility. A genius and prodigy, some call him the Christian Aristotle so far reaching and profound are his rational writings on Christ, the sacraments, penance, the Eucharist, communion for children, and the *Pange Lingua* sung at adoration. His crowning achievement, the *Summa Theologica*, written in a clear question/answer format, is the masterpiece of Catholic theology. He loved the epistles of St. Paul, and Saints Peter and Paul appeared to him as well as the Blessed Virgin Mary helping him with translation, and assuring him that his writings were acceptable to God. As a Doctor of the Church, he is the patron saint of universities, Catholic schools, and students.

Born a few centuries later in France, and living at the time of the Protestant Reformation and St. Vincent de Paul, the great St. Francis de Sales, also of an aristocratic family, dedicated his life to preaching and writing. He was responsible for sweeping conversions of tens of thousands who came to hear him preach, and his writings were no less persuasive to religious and laity alike. His many theological works had a passionate tone to them as he emphasized the joy of knowing Christ, and the great love of a God who saves. His famous work, *Introduction to the Devout Life*, begun as a series of letters to the common people, showed them how they too could be holy in the busy secular world by frequently turning their mind to prayer throughout the day in the form of simple aspirations. Despite his popular career as a priest, he too remained humble. Today many lay and religious orders are founded upon him. He is the patron saint of teachers, journalists, and deafness.

But before them lived St. Paul, apostle, martyr, pillar of our faith, and the first great theological writer. We hear at Mass in many of the second readings his convincing words wrought with authority, and his personal greetings to the diverse groups of the early church that he writes to assure them that Jesus Christ is God, and that all can be saved. His words are so passionate, poetic, and breathless that if we listen to them we are left rapt with joy. No doubt his dramatic conversion to Christ imbued his writings with that life-giving energy that comes from conversion. Lent is a great time to read these epistles as a whole and to listen wholeheartedly to them at Mass. Paul's letters were for the Romans, Ephesians, Corinthians, and Timothy and for us! He is the patron saint of popes and the lay apostolate, and writers, publishers, and the truth. The feast of his conversion is January 25.

We celebrate the anniversaries of these three great saints who all have a wonderful talent in common—that of writing, and its power of conversion. At the end of his life, St. Thomas Aquinas heard a voice from a crucifix ask him what he would like as a reward for "Thou has written well of me." I think we know his answer to that. You can do it too. Write to someone and convert him or her with love. It doesn't have to be a book, a treatise, or an epistle. A love note will suffice.

THE FEAST OF THE PRESENTATION OF THE LORD IN THE TEMPLE: GOD FROM GOD, LIGHT FROM LIGHT

FEBRUARY 2

The Presentation of Jesus in the Temple is the fourth of the Joyful Mysteries of the rosary and is described in the Gospel of St. Luke. On this day, as required by Jewish law, the firstborn was brought to the temple to be dedicated to the Lord, and the mother purified after the birth. Prior to Vatican II, this day was called the Feast of the Purification of Mary, but now the emphasis has returned to Jesus. It is also called Candlemas day, the day when all the candles used in the liturgical year are blessed. According to the calendar year it is Groundhog Day. Candlemas day, like Groundhog Day, was also used to predict the duration of winter, and the coming of spring.

Apart from honoring Jesus, the Feast of the Presentation has relevance to us as well. For many, our "presentation" was our Baptism as a child, when those sacramental waters healed the rift between God and man. Our parents and sponsors promised to guide us in our spiritual development, and made our baptismal vows of renunciation of sin and Satan for us, or as a baptized adult we made those promises. Throughout the liturgical year we have numerous occasions at Mass to publicly renew our baptismal vows, most notably on Easter and throughout the Easter season. Every time we go to church is a physical presentation to the Lord of ourselves, and notably if we know how to pray, our prayer is a presentation too.

There are many types of prayer—prayers of thanksgiving, adoration, petition, and contrition. In this prayerful encounter with God we talk to him who listens, and he talks to us, and we hopefully listen. Prayer is an indispensable part of our daily lives, and there are unlimited ways we can pray throughout the day that will infuse our lives with its holy power. We can start with a morning offering of thanksgiving in our own words to offer up the day to God's will, a noontime Angelus or rosary to regain and maintain our balance, a midday aspiration of contrition for Jesus' suffering, and completing the cycle with an evening prayer of adoration, petition, and thanksgiving. Sound like a lot of prayer? Not really. It is as normal as eating or brushing our teeth or any of the repetitive actions we perform as part of our day. Even Jesus, God, was constantly in prayer with his father. Prayer is conversation and communication. Let's talk and listen!

The pure beeswax candles that will accompany our liturgies will be blessed today, and whether the groundhog sees his shadow or not, we know that spring will come with its return of life to the earth. Lent will be here soon. The Paschal candle will be blessed at the Easter vigil, symbolizing Christ, as the light of the world, for without him, there is no light or no life.

The final time Jesus will be presented to his father is when he dies on the cross, and commends his spirit to his father as an act of obedience, completing what began with the presentation. We too must die to sin as St. Paul exhorts. Let us get ready for this penitential, healing, liturgical season by renewing our presentation to the Lord through prayer. Light a small candle in the midst of the February winter as the sun slowly obeys nature's rules and returns. Let it mark your vigil of cultivating a new prayer life. Visualize the Paschal candle, once lit through a prism by the sun, which will be lit at the Easter Vigil, and the incandescence of the true light of the world, the face of Jesus.

OUR LADY OF LOURDES AND WORLD DAY OF THE SICK: MASTER THE ONE YOU LOVE IS ILL (JOHN 11:3)

FEBRUARY 11 (MAY BE DURING LENT)

It is a Saturday morning in a walk-in clinic in January. There is standing room only. People look tired, pale, and unanimated. Who wants to be here on a first-come first-serve basis with other sick patients coughing and wheezing? Old and young, newborn, teens and adults are gathered together. A baby plaintively cries in discomfort; an old woman hobbles into the exam room on her leash of oxygen; a man holds his head in his hands, his grief disguised as a cold. Illness has no age or geographic boundaries. It's no fun being sick, and yet we are, and it is a very hard thing.

If you asked Catholics what is the most famous place for healing in the world their answer would undoubtedly be Lourdes. Lourdes, France has always had a strong association with those who are ill due to the spring that the Virgin revealed to Bernadette when Mary appeared to the young girl in one of her eighteen visits in 1858. Its healing properties for both spiritual and physical illness are so ingrained in our consciousness that it seems like this story is much more than one hundred and fifty years old, such is the power of Mary's visitations, and the cures that have been documented there. The connection of Mary with her son is truly inseparable, and so to appreciate Lourdes is to appreciate the value of the life that Christ gives us. Bernadette, poor, ill, and uneducated had the perfect poverty of body and spirit to accept the gift of Lourdes, and bring it to the world.

We can't all go to Lourdes or even afford to buy the holy water from the spring, but we do have a place to go. Perhaps the best-kept "secret" of some churches is the underemphasized liturgy that happens every First Friday at the conclusion of eucharistic adoration—benediction. Remember the incense, the golden monstrance, the words *Tantum ergo* (Down in Adoration Falling) from the *Pange Lingua*? When you go to benediction, the reverence and awe, majesty and mystery of childhood days is unveiled as it was for Bernadette in the grotto. We are in the presence of the eternal life-giving God of our creation and salvation. We are made humble and healed by his holy gaze. The only pilgrimage needed is to go to the chapel with an open heart.

Economic reports claim that the best professions to enter right now are those connected with health care, for like the poor, the sick will always be with us. Most of us are not looking for a new career. Going back to school or entering such a profession for the first time are certainly possibilities for some, but without that huge undertaking we can all care for the sick, whether the person has the common cold, arthritis, or cancer. Bringing the hope, faith, and love of Lourdes to others in their suffering is more important than going there. The message of Lourdes, and the message of the Eucharist, is the same. It is healing. It is love.

THE FEAST OF SAINTS CYRIL, METHODIUS, AND VALENTINE: GO OUT TO THE WORLD

FEBRUARY 14 (MAY BE DURING LENT)

On this date we probably think more of valentines, roses, and chocolate than brothers Saints Cyril and Methodius. In fact we may not even think of St. Valentine, third century martyr under the Roman Empire, anymore either. Perhaps this is because he like other legendary saints were removed in 1969 from the church calendar for liturgical veneration due to uncertainties about them, but they remain in the official list of saints. There have been several St. Valentines who were bishops and martyrs and whose feast days occur later in the year. As people so renowned they have made their mark on sacred and secular culture, and they are represented and honored in religious art, mosaics, and reliquaries in Italy, Spain, Jerusalem, Ireland, France, Austria, the United Kingdom and Switzerland.

For the last forty years Saints Cyril and Methodius have been assigned the date of February 14 in the church calendar, replacing Valentine. These two brothers were born into a political family in the 800s in Thessalonica, a part of Greece, and served professionally as administrators. Cyril was known as Constantine until almost the end of his life when he became a monk. Both became missionaries to the Ukraine, and Cyril helped form the Russian alphabet by modifying Greek.

These brothers were early proponents of the liturgy and church works being celebrated and translated into the vernacular, and fought on many political and ecclesiastical levels, suffering exile and illness, to bring the word of God to the Slavic people in their own language. Prior to this and then up until Vatican II, Greek and Latin were the official languages of the church. Cyril and Methodius recognized the power of language, and the freedom and identity it confers to a people by its ability to shape reality, and make participation in church life more meaningful. Methodius, who became a bishop and lived beyond his brother's time, translated almost the entire Bible and the works of the church into Slavonic. They laid the foundation for Christianity in the East and were named co-patrons of Europe by Pope John Paul II in 1980, receiving this unique title with St. Benedict of Nursia, St. Catherine of Siena, St. Bridget of Sweden and St. Teresa Benedicta of the Cross (Edith Stein).

Saints Valentine, Cyril, and Methodius wouldn't mind sharing this date in common. Separated by centuries, divided by countries, united by love of nation, God and fellow man, they spoke the same language of a loving God.

5

Lent and Easter

The baptismal font in Lent: crown of thorns
constructed of choia wood

AN OVERVIEW

As we begin the Lenten season, we recall the three important practices that define Lent: prayer, fasting, and almsgiving, but the greatest of these is charity Jesus said. To support almsgiving, the parish may designate baskets in the main church or the Blessed Sacrament chapel for the collection of non-perishable food items from Ash Wednesday through Holy Thursday. By giving to the needy. We respond to the summons, "For I was hungry and you gave me food" (Matt 25:35).

Catholics are obliged to fast on Ash Wednesday and Good Friday. This means that Catholics who are eighteen to fifty-nine years old are required to keep a limited fast, that is, to eat a single, normal meal, and have lesser meals as long as they do not add up to a second meal. Children are not required to fast. Those with medical conditions requiring greater or more regular food intake may be dispensed from this requirement.

Catholics are required to abstain from meat on Ash Wednesday, Good Friday, and all the Fridays of Lent. This applies to Catholics who are fourteen years or older. A person with special dietary needs may be dispensed from this requirement. But Lent is so much more than fasting or abstaining from food. It is the journey of Christ through his passion to the resurrection that we too must take. Let us try to understand and partake of this through these readings and the practice of these teachings.

Depending on the liturgical year, Lent can begin as early as February 4 or as late as March 10.

FASTING, ABSTINENCE, AND ALMSGIVING: BUT WHEN YOU GIVE ALMS, DO NOT LET YOUR LEFT HAND KNOW WHAT YOUR RIGHT IS DOING SO THAT YOUR ALMSGIVING MAY BE IN SECRET (MATT 6: 3-4)

The three cardinal benchmarks of Lent are prayer, fasting/abstinence, and almsgiving. Maybe this year almsgiving can take a different form of expression at your church where a more private form is encouraged.

Most of us grew up with the idea of giving up something for Lent. Usually this has translated into giving up a personal pleasure such as candy, chocolate, the movies, or some other favorite thing. Liturgically, the church fasts from flowers, elaborate music, singing the *Gloria*, and even the administration of some of the sacraments. Such acts of self-denial are functional and appropriate so that we can strip down to basics as is reflected in the sparse yet symbolically rich worship environment.

Lenten resolutions are a lot like New Year's ones. They are hard to keep because we tend to identify and pick those behaviors we think we should change but have a hard time doing. The idea of giving something up was meant to encompass not necessarily forfeiting an indulgence, but doing something through self-giving. Here is a chance to do something weekly in a new, imaginative, and less punitive way.

Put a dollar or more in your church envelope, pick a charity to support, give a homeless person food, money or clothing without their solicitation, visit someone sick or housebound, write to a prisoner or a soldier, go to the St. Vincent de Paul thrift store and donate good quality clothing and household gifts and groceries, work in a soup kitchen, join a charitable group or a parish ministry, or talk to a veteran. We can give money or food to someone instead of using it for ourselves. Give arms.

Fasting and abstinence in modern life and a culture of abundance is a concept we may find hard to relate to. If we are substituting lobster, shrimp, fish, and even great vegetable dishes for meat, where is the sacrifice? But eating a simple meal, or going without food every time we are hungry in mid-afternoon or before bed is something we can do, and self-control is good. Pure energy on many levels is derived from fasting.

Anyone who visits the church and particularly those who participate in our liturgy see that we are a church rich in spirit, music, art, generosity, talent, and support. The possibilities of fasting, abstinence, and almsgiving are as unlimited as our eternal spirit. Leave yours at the foot of the cross as he did. Lift up your heart to the Lord!

ASH WEDNESDAY: COME BACK TO THE LORD WITH ALL YOUR HEART; LEAVE THE PAST IN ASHES (JOEL 2:13)

Easter sometimes comes early, fast on the heels of Christmas, and maybe that is good to remind us of the constant presence of God in our lives, and to help us continue during Lent the joyful repentance and anticipation begun in Advent. This way we can seamlessly contemplate the mystery of the Incarnation as we head towards its fulfillment at the resurrection. Birth, death, and resurrection are not disparate events but part of the same mystery.

This week Lent begins. Ash Wednesday launches our turning to the Lord on the journey towards the immortality of Easter. The sacramental palms of triumphal glory and rejoicing from last Palm Sunday complete their cycle of transformation too. Burned to ashes and marked on our forehead in the sign of the cross, they remind us of the emptiness of the body without its integral, eternal spirit.

Born from the dust of volcanoes and the inside of stars, we were fashioned and infused with the breath of life from the hand of God who wanted to share his eternal life and love with us. Simple chemicals, the stuff of life, house the immortal spirit that allows our life and consciousness to be expressed and fulfilled through their union with Jesus when we die and return to the Lord.

Ashes are all around us, reminders of our seeming mortality. Ashes from wildfires that cripple communities, scorch states, destroy homes, landscapes and families forever abound and shock us into reality on the nightly news. Ashes from last night's lively fire that warmed us have now cooled. Ashes from volcanic eruptions that reshape cities and countries force us to recognize the important things, and invoke the resiliency of the human spirit to start over.

Interestingly, Ash Wednesday is one of the best-attended Masses of the year, many times with standing room only for the congregation who anticipate receiving the ashes, almost as if we crave them. The assembly comes forward with humility, embarrassment, emotion, reflection, and sadness in this combined private and public act of identification with the church and Christ.

The body is not bad. It is imbued with the spirit that allows the Holy Spirit to work in the world. It will rise again in a glorified form. The resurrection of the body can begin now through its purification by the fires and crosses and trials of life that will make us as pure as the palms reduced to ashes, to their essence.

As we come forward to receive the mark of our faith, the sign of the cross made by the black ashes, we can be somber and silent. But when they are received we can be joyful too. There is no reason to be a "sullen saint." We have been saved through the cross and the resurrection. Let us exalt in the cross of the ashes.

ASH WEDNESDAY: WHY ARE YOU SO DOWNCAST MY SOUL, WHY DO YOU GROAN WITHIN ME? (ALTERNATIVE VERSION) (PS 42:6)

The liturgical year, marking the history of our rich spiritual lives, consists of the liturgies of the church's life. As co-creators of an incomplete world, we select, standardize, and share in the feasts, solemnities and celebrations that constitute the liturgy of the Roman Catholic Church. Year after year we repeat its familiar themes of Advent, Christmas, Lent, Easter and Ordinary Time and all the events and feasts that flow between them, becoming reawakened and renewed with their familiar rhythm, hopefully never tiring of their significance. As saints and songs have proclaimed, "Let heaven and nature sing." The presence of God permeates everything.

Christmas is a past memory and it's Lent again, a period similar in many respects to Advent. In both seasons we are joyfully, hopefully, and penitentially awaiting Jesus in his incarnation and his resurrection respectively. Lent is longer, and we feel its sorrowful side more acutely, as we know the end of the story and the suffering Jesus must endure for us in order for new life to come. Like Advent and even Ordinary Time, the Lenten season will have weekly Gospel themes, but is helpful to look at each liturgical season as a whole period, and the weekly events as instructional stepping-stones that help us reach their culmination.

There is some freedom within liturgical planning for subjects unique to the congregation in a particular place, like music in Spanish or teen music, street processions and Indian dancers, and food collections and font decorations. These embellishments are allowed to involve the parish in their unique historical connection with God. Yet the universality of the Mass and the liturgical calendar in the Catholic Church makes it possible to worship God in a familiar way in every part of the world where the church is established. Most of us have been through Lent over and over as the liturgical year repeats itself, and so we have our conceptions of what it is. But there is a reason that the calendar comes around and around just like the days melt into night, and the winter blossoms into spring. It is a chance for us to deepen our faith, to feel and understand in a richer way the cycle of life, so profound are its mysteries.

Looking through the Lenten lens, we see that Lent like Advent is more than just waiting for Jesus' birth or resurrection, which has already come, or the promise of our rebirth or resurrection, for as Paul tells us, our resurrection has already occurred. The apostles who followed Jesus in his public ministry, through the garden and supper of Holy Week had no idea what was in store for them, and yet they followed him like the magi who pursued the celestial star. They were in Lent, just as we need to be, accompanying Jesus in the fulfillment of his mission by daily living of the Gospel, suffering alongside him, rejoicing when the tomb is found empty, when we recognize him at the end of the journey to Emmaus, in the breaking of the bread, or on the road to Damascus.

Lent is more than just giving up simple pleasures, wearing ashes, eating fish, and going to the Stations of the Cross. These are all external signs of our faith and they are good. But what about the internal signs? Take some time before Ash Wednesday comes and think about Lent. What has it been for you in the past? What was hard about it, natural, fulfilling, disappointing? What would you like it to be this year? Do you have a notion, a goal, or will you let it unfold? Will it be a solitary period, or one shared with others? Do you see your resurrected body now? What do you need to go through to get there? Eventually we will wash off the ashes and resume the sacrifices we enacted. How will Lent have changed us by us having changed Lent?

LENT AND ENVIRONMENT: LORD SEND OUT YOUR SPIRIT, AND RENEW THE FACE OF THE EARTH (RESPONSORIAL PSALM BASED ON PS 104:29)

If landscape possesses the ability to shape consciousness, perhaps few places can compare with the rugged natural beauty of New Mexico, where the mind expands, the body matures, and the soul is inspired to reach out beyond the piñons, the interminable blue mountain skies, and the very starkness of the terrain, to the God of creation. That consciousness is expressed in its art, architecture, and outlook. In this unique tri-cultural nexus there is a place where a multi-colored palette creates a living canvas by blending the beauty of native traditions, art, stories, food, and music. In a geographic area that acutely acknowledges the interdependence of resources like water and earth, sun and snow, mountains and wind, we are poised to understand the delicate balance of nature. But wherever we live we have an opportunity for creating life in balance through our social, mystical connection with each other, and the variability of creation. The world is a beautiful gift and we are its caretakers.

While the focus of liturgy is on the inside, meaning the inside the church and our soul, there is a beautiful natural liturgy that plays itself out in the environment, what we could call the liturgy of the natural world. Here we can see that the needs of the person are also the needs of the planet; we are inextricably connected to it. While the emphasis in the church is on personal sin, there is also a broader social sin. The first social sin is what we call original sin that began with Adam and Eve, when not only did they ostracize themselves from God by choosing to be God through their disobedience, but their choice affected all of mankind. Theirs was an act with social and spiritual consequences, resulting in the expulsion from the glorious Garden of Eden. We would not have done otherwise. Now only passing through the Garden of Gethsemane will restore that paradise.

Pope Benedict XVI has spoken in homilies, books, and teachings revealing his environmental perspective about this concept of social sin in his ecological, "green," messages in which he uses Roman Catholic doctrine to explain and expand such sin to include the things we do as a culture, a nation, or the world that harm the precious resources of creation. Environmentally conscious lifestyles, he points out, are a moral responsibility, and a lack thereof one of the "new" deadly sins.

As Lent progresses, follow the vertical purple banners on the church columns that direct our eyes upward, and take a good look at the real thorns of the northern New Mexico countryside that wither life which are placed in the center of the baptismal font and by the *ambo* (place where the Gospel is read). Look at the red breasted birds waiting patiently on a bare cherry tree for spring blossoms, a solitary rabbit that comes out with the sun to scratch for tender grass, a deer waking at dawn, and the beer cans and plastic bags that litter a back road or a highway. Think what you, what we can do to assist in the fashioning of the unfinished world that we are invited to participate in. Nature nourishes, liturgy nurtures, and relationship renews. God is the origin and the common denominator.

THE LITURGICAL ENVIRONMENT FOR LENT: FOR WITH YOU IS THE FOUNTAIN OF LIFE AND IN YOUR LIGHT WE SEE LIGHT (PS 36:10) (ALTERNATIVE VERSION)

With few exceptions the Lenten liturgical environment has a flavor different from the rest of the year. From Ash Wednesday to Holy Thursday the familiar themes of purple and desert, rocks and thorns, baskets for food collections, empty holy water fingerbowls, and the unadorned baptismal font stand in sharp contrast to the extravagance of proud Easter lilies, and the riot of red and white poinsettias announcing the Incarnation at Christmas. Now amidst the apparent barrenness and dearth of decoration is a bare yet rich setting that strips the church down to basics. Through these symbols we sacrifice the beauty and comfort of flowers and plants, our longing for music and singing, to focus on the emptiness of our interior life without the saving grace of Christ. This change makes all the more poignant the preparation, repentance, purification, and renewal that need to occur in us as individuals and as a church so that we can participate in the greatest of all our holy days, Easter, when the promise of eternal life, as fulfilled in the Resurrection, is offered to us.

Lent is a journey and it begins as soon as we enter the church and mindfully bless ourselves with the sign of the cross. That simple, humble gesture is profound in significance—a mini-purification in which we recommit ourselves to our baptismal promises that allow us to enter into the fullness of Christ. The linear, regal, penitential violet swags adorning the columns or architecture connect earth to heaven, directing us to lift up our hearts, prayers, and petitions to God for forgiveness. The heavy, cumbersome wooden cross that literally may be divided for Good Friday adoration and is carried by the faithful, allows us to enter into the finality of Christ's suffering as we trip and stumble towards the altar and are humbly transformed by its weight and grace. Dried grape vines fashioned into wreaths surround the candles at the altar like crowns. They appear apparently dead, but slowly sprout moss, buds for *Laetare* Sunday, and finally, the glory of Easter flowers.

But the Baptismal font, the site throughout the year for tourists' admiration and curiosity and yearly baptisms, is truly the central focus of our liturgical journey. It is not just for the elect who will be baptized at Easter but for all of us to reflect on our Baptism and its significance in our lives. Amongst the thorns and dry winter woods flows the water of everlasting life that is always with us even as Christ promised he would always be with his church. Just as the font is the center of the Advent liturgy, evoking our longing and anticipation for Christ's coming, even more so during Lent it is the center of hope for our redemption through its cleansing, clear, holy waters.

The Lenten liturgical environment should assist us in using Lent as an important vehicle for spiritual growth. Coordinate your life with the mournful, lonely beat of a drum as the cross is carried, reflect on the healing capacities of dryness and water, let the cacti and the sorrowful violet create in you a pure and longing heart so that the incomprehensible glory of the Resurrection, expressed in candles and linens, flowers and song take us to a new level as the Body of Christ.

LENT AND PRAYER THROUGH THE LENS OF MARK AND PAUL: I HAVE SEEN THE LORD (JOHN 20:18)

In the liturgical year of the Gospel of Mark, called Year B, it is fitting to look at Mark's recounting of the events of the Lenten season so we can view his perspective through his holy eye and word.

As the oldest and shortest of the Gospels, the Gospel of Mark has the focused, triune message of Jesus as God, forgiveness as paramount, and the "cross" as the way to salvation. While the Jews certainly spent their history on and are still waiting for the Messiah, their concept of him never supposed that he would actually be the son of God; perhaps that is why they could not recognize Jesus when he came. In Mark's sixteen chapters, half are devoted to Christ's journey from Jerusalem to his death, thus showing the centrality and significance of the passion narrative, which is found in all four Gospels, unlike every New Testament theme.

In contrast to Mark's brevity, over half of the New Testament comes from Paul. Similar to Mark, the message of Paul is urgent. Paul's letters expounded on the suffering and death of Jesus as the means of our salvation, but he overflows with the joy of the resurrection. Resurrection was a topic alluded to in the Old Testament books and traditions, which were not standardized at the time, with various understandings of resurrection, from the impersonal resurrection of a nation, to a resurrection of only the good, to the resurrection of all. Yet its significance was never developed, understood or accepted by all Jews. Until Jesus came, making all mankind his heirs, who could imagine God taking on human form or even rising from the dead! When we meet Jesus personally as Paul did the living Christ, the scales fall off of our eyes; reality is totally changed with Jesus Incarnate.

Thirty years before the Gospels were written they were the oral "good news," "good announcement," and "the message of salvation," conveyed through preaching. These core beliefs were heard, processed, and assimilated by the receivers, and then later recorded. Today we have the opportunity to experience the Gospels this way at Mass, and with the benefits of technology. To reinstitute the practice of listening to the Gospel, Bible CDs are useful to listen to as the Good News made available in modern times.

We listen to music, the news, television, in fact most of our sensory experiences relate to hearing. Lent is a good time to begin the practice of Bible study. Listen to it alone, with family, daily or weekly, setting aside special time to allow its word to surround and descend upon you like the comfort of the Holy Spirit without the stress of visual reading. At Mass, put down the missal, and listen to the first and second readings and the Gospel. Experience scripture. But if hearing is difficult as it is for many of our society, hear through the eyes of your heart as you read the words from the missal as they are proclaimed as if for the very first time. Let us hear from Mark, "Truly this man was the Son of God" (Mark 15:39), and rejoice with Paul—do you not realize that Jesus Christ is in you?

THE SCRIPTURES OF LENT: THE WORD OF THE LORD. THANKS BE TO GOD.

The Sunday Gospels of Lent abound with stories of the public life of Jesus. In this period, these images are some of the most intense, memorable Gospel passages that we joyously recollect when hear them again as a familiar account that Jesus is God.

The emphasis on Jesus' public ministry is understandable at this point in time. Copious sins are forgiven, miracles performed, and the momentum builds up for his entry into Jerusalem, and then his passion and death. It is a record crammed with miracles of physical, mental and spiritual healing, and even the raising of the dead of the most unlikely of people, not even Jesus' people, but strangers and foreigners, who by virtue of their belief in him are invited to share in the kingdom. All of this is designed to fulfill the scriptures that he is the ultimate prophet, the messiah, the son of God, come to expand the covenantal promises to all.

In the Gospel from Luke, we see Jesus frequently in prayer as a model for our lives. He is tempted by the devil, but dispels him, and then is radiantly transfigured before his apostles, in both instances establishing his hierarchy over heaven and earth. In the third through the fifth Sundays of Lent, the Gospel from John, chosen to coincide with the Rites of Christian Initiation of Adults (RCIA), we are reacquainted with the Samaritan woman at the well, who is promised living water, the blind man whose sight is restored, and then Lazarus raised from the dead. They are the same promises made to us as well of the life we will find in Christ. We can be healed by exemplifying the unquestioning faith, unassuming humility, and spontaneous and public testimonies of witness like these figures in the Gospels.

The first and second readings prior to the Gospel contain similar themes. In the first readings, we have vivid confessions of faith from Moses and Abram; images of anointing and bones dry without life. In the second readings from Paul he reminds us that we can become new, and how necessary this is. And like Paul, who persecuted Christians and Jesus himself, we can convert, and be reconciled to God.

We see and listen to the word of God at Mass, letting the words proclaimed enter our eyes and ears, impacting our minds, and changing our hearts, and that is an important communal, spiritual experience, the Liturgy of the Word. Reading the Word of God in the Bible privately is a deeply personal encounter as our eyes take in the poetic, mysterious written word from the prophets, the evangelists, and God himself. Both acts are rich blessings of our Catholic faith, and the covenant he has established with his people for all time.

LENTEN PRAYER: FOREVER I WILL SING, THE GOODNESS OF THE LORD (RESPONSORIAL PSALM BASED ON PS 89:2)

We go to church, the house of the Lord, to worship him. Prayer is the vehicle for that worship. There are many types of prayer. The liturgical worship environment should facilitate worship and participation through prayer. Certainly the structure of the Mass provides the opportunity for community prayer through the responsorial psalms, the Kyrie, the Gloria, the Creed, the Our Father, and other acclamations, as well as periods for private reflection.

Perhaps second to verbal prayer, we share our worship of God through music. Truly no voice is unpleasing to God. Bilingual communities may use Spanish, Polish, Hawaiian or other languages in addition to English in their liturgies. To give all the opportunity to lift up their voice in sung prayer, the parish should provide worship aids, hymnals or song sheets.

At Lent we are afforded special opportunities for prayer. Retreats are unique events that evoke prayerful reflection on a spiritual theme. Generally they involve attending a series of sermons by a thoughtful and inspiring priest, and are an intensely communal and personal experience.

The church at Lent formally offers the Stations of the Cross. They are a special and heartfelt way to follow Jesus from his condemnation to his death. Jesus falls repeatedly in his suffering and then dies. Who are we to complain? Stations are held every Friday in the early evening. Try to go to Stations of the Cross at least once in Lent or make a personal Stations of the Cross, and travel with him through his passion. Spend extra time at the station that has the most meaning for you that day and pray.

Reading the Bible is a wonderful way to be quiet and still so that the word of God can speak to us. Each year is a different cycle of the Gospel readings. During Lent, put aside a special time, such as Sunday evening before bed or a Friday night after dinner to read a section, from beginning to end, of the account of Jesus' life in the cyclical Gospel of the year.

In some parishes, there may be a unique liturgical feature, such as the carrying of the cross at the start of Mass to the beat of a drum. This is a powerful and startling meditative and visual prayer. The cross is very heavy; the drum, a slow and fading heart beat. Some parishioners like this, others don't. It slows our consciousness, our hearts, freezes the moment, and transports us in time to Calvary. Analyze how it impacts you. Can we pick up the cross and go there? We need to. There is no escaping its paradoxical promise.

And so, prayer has many expressions, both verbal and non-verbal. It is ultimately a behavior, sometimes formal, sometimes communal or alone, sometimes silent, sometimes vocal, sometimes heart wrenching, sometimes joyous, said out loud, whispered, or sung and in postures of kneeling, genuflection, bowing, sitting, standing, prostration, walking, with hands folded or outstretched. But in the end, all prayer is conversation with the God of creation, the God of life and unconditional love, the

God for whom we were created and who suffered and died to save us. This Lent and forever, let us pray.

LENT AND FASTING: THEY TESTED GOD IN THEIR HEARTS BY DEMANDING THE FOOD THEY CRAVED (PS 78:18)

Fasting has gone out of fashion. In an economy of relative abundance and fast food lifestyles, we don't really think fasting does that much good for our soul. Apart from religious traditions, in a culture that promotes immediate gratification, we don't see the relevance and the importance of giving things up, although the cultivation of willpower is a valuable skill and a meaningful sacrifice. It is true that giving up a meal or a treat that can then be satisfied in another form has no purpose. One area we could explore as an avenue of fasting is to give up our addictions.

At first glance most of us might not think that we have any addictions. Aren't those the things other people have like addictions to alcohol or drugs? An addiction is anything, any behavior or preoccupation that enslaves us, that gets in the way of our relationship with and our reliance upon God. These actions can include virtually anything: our need to have the last word; our compulsive internet behaviors and e-mails; our requirement for information and entertainment; our emotional unkindness, cruelty or criticism of another; gossip; our concern with how we look, our prestige, status or money; our obsession to always keep busy or to do nothing; our piety, pride, and unforgiveness. There are no shortages of any social, environmental, mental, behavioral or physical deed that kills our body and soul, that attempts to fill our emptiness by denying our dependence on where God rightly fits into our lives.

In March we honor two towering saints who understood the nature of fasting, St. Joseph and St. Patrick. Both men, living five hundred years apart, had many things in common, some of which was their humility to be attentive to dreams, and their visitation by angels summoning them to be led by the hand of God. Joseph, as the obedient stepfather to Jesus, made Christ's life and the beginning of the church possible; Patrick as an ardent bishop brought the Gospel outside the boundaries of the Greco-Roman world to the slaves, barbarians, and outcasts of Ireland thus making the church truly Catholic (universal). To Patrick, prayer, fasting, and penance were integral parts of his life. For forty days he ensconced himself on a mountain to make special prayers for Ireland, surrounded by demons so dense there was no visibility, until he vanquished them with his sweet sounding bell that blessed his country. Joseph's strong, steadfast, silent devotion to Jesus and Mary surely took the form of prayer and fasting from even the most common expectations and pleasures for the sake of his family.'

Like Patrick and Joseph, we can give up things that make space for God. So go ahead, have that chocolate if it will make you sweeter. Keep the behaviors that help you respond to God and each other, and throw off the ones that are tired, dry, and worn like the old wineskins of Matthew's Gospel.

THE CATECHUMENS AND THE LITURGY: WHOM ARE YOU LOOKING FOR? (JOHN 20:15)

Now that the church environment is aesthetically and prayerfully prepared to provide both the backdrop and the instrument for reinforcing worship, we turn our attention to why we gather as a church, that is, liturgy. Derived from the Greek *leitourgia*, the word "liturgy" literally means, "work of the people," with that work being the public ritual of prayer and adoration. In the next weeks of Lent, the focus of the church is on the treasury of the Lenten liturgy, which culminates in the passion, death, and resurrection of Christ during Holy Week.

Throughout the years we as Catholics repeat the Lenten rhythm of renewal as our legacy on earth to prepare for Easter. It is a necessary time in our spiritual development to renew our relationship with God through the practices of prayer, fasting/abstinence and almsgiving. It is befitting that experiencing this Lenten journey with us are those undertaking the Rites of Initiation—Baptism, Confirmation, and Holy Eucharist. The *catechumens* also referred to as the *elect* after their Rite of Election during Lent, take their final steps towards Baptism, and are then confirmed and receive Holy Eucharist. Accompanying us also are the *candidates* (those baptized in another faith), and the *confirmandi* (those baptized in the Catholic Church), who now receive through Confirmation the outpouring of grace through the gifts of the Holy Spirit, thus completing the grace begun at Baptism. They are now welcomed into full communion with the church. The infants and children, singularly but no less significantly, receive Baptism, which marks the beginning of their new life in Christ.

Unless we attend the Easter Vigil or the Sunday Masses during Lent when they are gathered weekly, we may wonder or even forget about their parallel journey with us. We may even ponder why their initiation is combined with Easter, although historically this initially was so, and even more for them than for us. But like the children, and adults, and their sponsors who use Lent as a period of preparation for their reception into the church at the Easter Vigil, we too renew our baptismal promises that same night and in the fifty day Easter period, reaffirming that we accept Christ into our lives and throw off the old self.

As a parish, an assembly, we are a community; we are a church, the People of God, traveling toward heaven through the door of Baptism. Let us walk together in the suffering, sorrows, and stillness of Lent to the invitation of the Paschal banquet, which we accepted at Baptism, made manifest in the Resurrection.

BAPTISM: I AM THE LIVING WATER (JOHN 4:11)

It may sit at the entrance of the church, in the center of the church, halfway between the entrance to the church and the altar, or to the side of the sanctuary. If you don't see it when you first come in the front doors, you do as you make your way to the altar.

Large white poinsettias surround it at Christmas; a garden of lilies, orchids and chrysanthemums christen it during the fifty-day post-Easter period. An Advent wreath may halo it before Christmas; gardenias float in it for the Chrism Mass. Cattails, reeds, sunflowers, and pine emerge from it at late summer liturgies. Red gladiolas blaze from the waters at Pentecost, and in the Lenten season it is crowned with thorns.

Its gentle running water can be heard during quiet moments at Mass. When the church is cleaned, coins may be retrieved from it, thrown in unknowingly by those who think it is a wishing well. Perhaps it is, except that the wish has already come true, more than we could ever imagine or understand! It is the baptismal font with its blessed water that confers Baptism into the church, the body of Christ, and everlasting life. It is central to the church, just as Baptism is the core of every subsequent sacrament, and the portal to paradise.

Babies are baptized there throughout the year. The adult, teen, and child catechumens are immersed into its holy water at the Easter vigil, and emerge reborn. At the start of the Easter vigil the newly lit paschal candle, the new fire, is plunged into the waters to consummate fire and water in a marriage of heaven and earth. At the Easter vigil Mass the holy water fonts are then filled with the new, blessed water.

Many stand at it in silence. Stop by the font and bless yourself with its cool, holy water. Feel the smooth stone from which its flows. Come to the Easter Vigil to be immersed in a liturgy at the heart of our faith. No pennies please (or any other coins), just a promise, cross your heart, in the sign of the cross, that Jesus is the center of your life.

LENT AND ALMSGIVING: GIVE THEM WHAT YOU HAVE . . . I WILL TAKE CARE OF EVERYTHING ELSE THAT IS NEEDED (MARK 6:37)

As the somberness of Lent coincides with the economic trials of our time, we can feel the burden of suffering and poverty. From Old Testament times to the period when the new church was just becoming established, and early Christians were martyred for their faith, many were convinced that the end of the world was imminent. Indeed some think that this is true today, with poverty and its accompanying social illnesses being some of those signs. One thing is certain, with more people in the world than ever before, there is more poverty now than in any time in history. Non-profit organizations report cupboards empty of food, and charities are experiencing decreased giving. The middle class is unaccustomed to material poverty, and so there is the temptation to turn inward and conserve. But the interesting thing is that volunteerism is up. Could this be what is important?

If we turn to sacred scripture we are comforted with the promises of a time when poverty will pass. From Nehemiah 9:15 we hear, "Food from heaven you gave them in their hunger, water from a rock you sent them in their thirst." Revelation 7:16 says, "They will not hunger or thirst anymore." "Blessed are you who hunger now, for you shall be satisfied," the Beatitudes promise (Luke 6:21). Even our beloved St. Paul boastfully wrote in his letters to the Corinthians in 2 Cor 11:27 of what he endured for Jesus and viewed it as his privilege, "I have labored and toiled and have often gone without sleep; I have known hunger and thirst and have often gone without food; I have been cold and naked."

Like the ashes on our forehead, Lent is traditionally marked by almsgiving. We are used to finding in our mail requests from charities in Africa, the Philippines, and other far off places asking for money for food, water, medicine, and education, but now the house that needs it may be our own, our friend's, family's or neighbor's. Unprecedented numbers of organizations are approaching our parishes for help with annual Lenten food collections, and others need meals prepared, and donations of toiletries, socks, and underwear, revealing the very transparency of our community's basic needs.

Pope Benedict XVI in his address on January 1, 2009, looking at the problem of poverty in the world, wisely proclaimed, "Humanity is one family in God." Poverty destroys the potential of every person, breeds violence, disease, despair and environmental contamination. We might personally be having a hard time now but almost one and a half billion people live in extreme poverty on less than a dollar and twenty-five cents a day, and half of these are children! Our situation cannot compare. "To fight poverty is to build peace," Benedict declares. Charity may begin at home, but it doesn't have to end there. The peace that comes from social justice can be in our midst.

Our President maintains that the purpose of government is to do for the people what we cannot do alone. Although not perfectly realized yet, all policies that promote the dignity and respect for life will be tools in the eradication of poverty, and the establishment of peace. All of us have to work towards these ends including the poor who want a meaningful life of work and hope. In the apparent contradictions that Jesus spoke of, we are all poor, and we are all rich if we work for the common good of our planet and each other. The simplicity and starkness of Lent can lead us to that clear conclusion.

Acting out of abundance creates abundance. In our collections this liturgical season, when you see the empty baskets at the foot of the sanctuary, or as the collection basket passes by, when you receive a charitable solicitation in the mail, or are asked to do something for someone else outside of your normal boundaries, act swiftly and naturally; the human heart was made to give and the Sacred Heart shows us how.

LENT AND THE OILS OF OUR FAITH: GO UP TO GILEAD, AND TAKE BALM (JER 46:11)

Oils are a precious gift. They are life giving to both the body and the soul, a veritable comfort. Oils are used for cooking and for eating, rich in their ability to nourish and impart vital nutrients in an immediate utilizable way. Oils are for cleansing and purging. They can lift impurities from the skin, and other organs, and make them function better. Oils are for relaxing. They soothe tired, tight muscles, restore elasticity to the worn body, brighten the skin, and offer physical refreshment. Oils are for hospitality and pleasure, their numerous scents uplifting and invigorating the body and the mind. Oils are for anointing thereby conferring a special status on the receiver. Oils are for illuminating, for lighting a lamp, for polishing wood, for lubricating, and smoothing friction. They are a luxurious necessity.

With so many natural functions, it is not surprising that oils are used in church liturgy. They have a long history in the Bible as a common medicine for physical and spiritual illnesses, and for the anointing of the sick and the dead. Oils were used to anoint priests and kings such as David, with that action considered equivalent to crowning, and symbolic of receiving the spirit of God to perform his tasks on earth.

Oils are used sacramentally to confer grace in four of our seven sacraments (Do you know which four?) Walk by the ambry, the glass case that houses the sacramental oils, and look at the rich, thick oils that are blessed every year at the Chrism Mass, and that are used throughout the liturgical year in the administration of those sacraments. "*Christ*" in Greek means the "anointed one," and the name of two of these blessed oils used for ordination of a bishop, and Confirmation and Baptism is *Chrism*, derived from Christ's name. It is also referred to as the oil of gladness. Prior to Easter, is the Chrism Mass when the sacramental oils are prepared and distributed to the archdiocese parishes for their liturgical use throughout the year.

This Sunday is *Laetare* Sunday, the Sunday of rejoicing in the midst of Lent. The church will have small signs of life within it. Go look at the delicate bird's nests, and flowering bulbs by the foot of the cross, in the front of the Paschal candle, and by the ambry, or wherever your church has added symbols for *Laetare* Sunday. They are a promise of the aromatic, sweet oils of daffodils, tulips, hyacinths, azaleas, and lilies that will fill the church on Easter. But before we get to Easter, is there anything in the way of keeping us from savoring the fullness of the oil as Jesus did when his feet and hair were anointed in the Gospels when he was in our company?

Easter is fast approaching. It is a good time to receive the Sacrament of Reconciliation. Forgiveness is like oil. Thicker than water and rich in nature, it can heal people, communities, and nations. Experience the healing grace that comes from reconciliation and rejoice!

THE CHRISM MASS AND THE HOLY OILS:
FOR I, THE LORD, AM YOU HEALER (EXOD 15:26)
(ALTERNATIVE VERSION)

The Chrism Mass, held annually in cathedral churches, is one of the most beautiful Masses to participate in due to its unique theme. *Chrism*, taken from the name Christ, means "anointing." This is an imposing Mass, when in addition to the core constituents of the Mass, its dual focus is the consecration by the bishop or archbishop of the sacred oils that will be used throughout the year in the administration of the sacraments, and the consecration and blessing of sacred things. It is the same occasion when the renewal of the priestly vows by the clergy of the archdiocese occurs. While this Mass can be said at any time of year, the Chrism Mass meshes naturally with Lent, and its emphasis on Baptism, and the presentation of the oils on Holy Thursday, and our promises of baptismal renewal made at Easter and in the Eastertide period.

Oils by nature are unctuous and soothing, nourishing, rich and enriching. They have been used culturally for cooking, lighting lamps, and healing muscles, and so are the symbolic, perfumed sacramental oils that confer the gifts of the Holy Spirit. There are three types of holy oils, all made with a rich olive oil base, and then infused with other natural herbs. The oil of the catechumens, also called the oil of salvation, is for Baptism, such as for those now called the elect who are baptized at the Easter Vigil. It has the function of cleansing from sin, and strengthening of spirit by making its imprint on the person. The oil of the sick is used in the Sacrament of the Anointing of the Sick, (what we used to call the Last Rites or Extreme Unction (Last Anointing), for the anointing of those who are ill or dying or about to undergo surgery, so that they are healed and comforted. The Chrism oil is distinct from the other oils in that it is mixed with an aromatic herb from the pine family called balsam. The use of balsam goes back to apostolic times. The Chrism oil is used for the sacrament of Confirmation and Holy Orders.

The Holy Oils are stored in beautiful bottles in a special place in the church called the ambry (locked cabinet). The ambry may be appropriately located close to the baptismal font and the Paschal candle. The oils are blessed by the presider and distributed to the priests to return to their parishes and to use in the ensuing year. Due to availability, convenience, proximity, or seating, not everyone has the opportunity to attend this solemn Feast of the Oils, however it is certainly one worth participating in if you can.

The laity, in addition to the priests and other religious as members of the Body of Christ, all share in his priesthood as baptized and confirmed Christians. We are called and commissioned by Christ to embody him to the world, anointed, and nourished by the oils of our faith.

FAITH IN THE DESERT: HER DESERTS HE SHALL MAKE LIKE EDEN, HER WASTELAND LIKE THE GARDEN OF THE LORD (ISA 51:3)

We understand dryness in the desert southwest or places where we experience drought. We accept the arid earth, the scanty landscape, and the promising blue skies even when water doesn't come. We love the sun and await its return. Even in the liturgy of song, we give thanks for the beneficent rains of summer, and the snows of winter, that bring the spring back to us. These are gifts of nature. Rain down.

We are both geographically and spiritually in the desert. Are we as aware of our spiritual dryness and its need for resolution as our climatic aridity? Do we invite the life-saving graces of God into our lives daily through morning, midday, or evening prayer? Do we sing at Mass and joyfully no less, participate in the sacraments frequently, say the rosary daily, rise above ritual in response to the risen Jesus amongst us through recommitted discipleship?

These are ways to renew our faith, strengthen our faith, develop our faith, live our faith—the faith of our fathers we may have been nourished in as a child, returned to after relinquishing, or neglecting, or blessed with as a gift in later life. Don't take it for granted. Faith is a tender, delicate shoot that wants to reach like a beanstalk to the sky. Cherish it, practice it, live it, read about it, share it, water it with the word of God, and feed it with the Body and Blood of his son, Jesus Christ.

The temptations of the desert are as real for us as they were for Jesus, so do not despair. Periods of physical deprivation, silence, and fasting give us strength. The spirit's needs are revealed, just as they were for Jesus when he emerged after forty days and nights in the desert. He then knew his life's purpose, and was ready to take up his cross, and complete the mission of his public life.

Do you really know what your life's purpose is? Has it just become a function of lifestyle and circumstances, or a conscious choice? Have you examined it? Do you want to change it, can you change it, and should you change it? Maybe we can't drop everything as the fishermen who became apostles did, but we can have the receptivity of the simple people in the scriptures who turned to God in faith: the dispossessed and possessed, the blind, ill, paralytics, lepers, lunatics, and common people who recognized his truth, and expressed their faith because they made room for him in their bodies, minds, and hearts. Faith is our response to God's plan for salvation. Think about this as the inwardness of winter and Lent draws to a close so we can bring our faith into the fullness of approaching summer and Ordinary Time.

The days in the desert of spiritual dryness are not up to us to end. God will give us what we need, and whether it is a dark night of the soul lasting one day, forty nights, or many years as it did for many saints, and even with St. Teresa of Calcutta for nearly her entire professed life. So pray for rain and spiritual, life–giving water. It will come, but we have to ask for it, pray for it, and make room for it in the dry desert of our hearts.

LAETARE SUNDAY: *LAETARE* JERUSALEM, O BE JOYFUL JERUSALEM

It is the fourth Sunday of Lent, known as *Laetare* Sunday, the Sunday of rejoicing. In the past it had been called Mid-Lent Sunday since Lent is halfway over. Because of this halfway mark, it was also called the Sunday of Refreshment, a day to rejoice and lighten up on Lenten restrictions with a reprieve from the things we gave up during Lent. It had been called Rose Sunday too, when now rose-colored vestments and altar cloths are used, replacing the reddish Roman purple that is used in the rest of Lent. Commemorating the miracle of the five loaves and fishes, it was referred to as the Sunday of the Five Loaves, but it has now retained within the Catholic Church the name *Laetare* for rejoice.

In the spirit of anticipation and rejoicing, flowering branches are brought into the church, hints of the fullness of Easter that approaches. It is a good time to assess how we are doing with our Lenten practices of prayer, fasting/abstinence, and almsgiving. Have we been faithful to them? Have we done anything different during Lent to utilize this special liturgical season for our joyful turning to the Lord on the journey towards Easter?

Today is a day to rejoice for the hope of the resurrection, the New Jerusalem, a place of peace where God reigns, and the Promised Land is reached. The Book of Revelations tells us that in that city there will be no more death. The earth and the heavens will pass away and God will dwell with his people forever. He will wipe away every tear; the old order will pass away. There will be no more mourning or wailing, pain or death, and God will dwell with his people forever, giving them life-giving water, the water of Baptism, by which all can be saved. He will rise as he said.

It is not too early to take a look at the rest of the liturgical period from now to Easter, as it will pass quickly. Mark off the holy days and events that you will attend to make Easter all it can be for you spiritually. Finish reading the Gospel of the year, go to the Sacrament of Reconciliation, and the Stations of the Cross, Eucharistic Adoration, and extra Masses and reconcile with those you don't want to forgive. Do something for him. Jesus has a wonderful Easter in store for you. Don't wait till Easter to rejoice. He is with us as he said.

LAETARE SUNDAY AND THE FEAST DAYS IN LENT— THE ANNUNCIATION AND THE FEAST OF ST. JOSEPH: REJOICE AND BE GLAD, YOURS IS THE KINGDOM OF GOD (JOHN 5:12) (ALTERNATIVE VERSION)

March 25 and 19 respectively

The fourth Sunday in Lent, *Laetare* Sunday, is the demarcation point for Lent being half over. *Laetare* means rejoice and we have much cause for rejoicing. That day is a brief respite, a glimpse of the glory to come. Jerusalem, the city of destiny of Christ's passion, death, resurrection, and ascension, the Holy City of salvation history, with all of its poignant pain, tenuous peace, and eternal promises, is in sight. We share in Jesus' longing and lamentation for it.

Lent and Advent of course are the not the same, but they do have shared characteristics of hope, preparation, and renewal that we just experienced at Christmas. *Laetare* Sunday is somewhat analogous to *Gaudete* Sunday in Advent. *Gaudete* also means rejoice, in this case for the coming of the Incarnation. On *Laetare* Sunday the church environment is modified in subtle ways from violet to dusky rose vesture, wistful, delicate spring buds, moss, and flowers. We are cognizant of the vulnerability of spring, nature, and the human condition.

In Lent we have the feasts of St. Joseph and the Annunciation, propitious occasions to remind us of the importance of the Holy Family in our lives. Mary's unequivocal "yes" to be the mother of God at the time of the angel's annunciation to her is a glorious occasion to be celebrated. St. Joseph's feast calls to mind his model of humility and perfection. It is good to honor them during this time. The *ordo* (small book of liturgical options) allows white, the color of solemnity and celebration to be used, and we need not fast from flowers on those days. The feast of St. Joseph, husband of Mary, is March 19 and the Annunciation is March 25.

At this juncture it is a good time to evaluate our Lenten practices and continue on with renewed strength as we look forward to Easter in less than a month. With our merciful and patient God we can always pick up and start over again. The Book of Tobit from the Old Testament contains wise maxims in regard to prayer, fasting, and abstinence, the Lenten trilogy of practices. "Prayer and fasting are good, but better than either is almsgiving accompanied by righteousness" (Tob 12:8). Now is a great time to continue to generously offer food to the needy in our donation baskets in the church before the end of Lent, or to give alms in other personal, meaningful ways.

All of these liturgical events are harbingers of new life, bountiful gifts of opportunity to us, as we trek forward from the exodus, from the desert, to our new life in Christ in the Eucharist, at Easter, and for all eternity.

PALM SUNDAY AND THE TRIDUUM:
AND I WILL RAISE YOU UP ON THE LAST DAY (JOHN 6:40)

In this our last Sunday of Lent, Jesus triumphantly enters into Jerusalem, bittersweet in its significance, for it heralds both the fulfillment of the prophecies, and man's reconciliation with God, and the week of his passion, death, and resurrection.

The regal, penitential purple of the sorrowful season, and the delicacy of *Laetare's* rose, are briefly punctuated with the red of royalty, blood, sacrifice, martyrdom, and mortality. Jesus, sitting on the diminutive, demure, and humble donkey, instead of a conquering horse, is greeted by the procession of palms, symbols of honor, and the exalted resurrection. In commemoration of his kingship, we are given blessed palms to keep in our homes to grace them until they become ashes again. "Lent," meaning "quarantine for a required, imposed period of isolation," the forty days in the ark, the forty years in the desert on the way to Canaan, the forty days Jonah warns Nineveh it has to repent, Christ's forty days in the desert, is almost over.

The week to come will be hard but holy and as utterly necessary for Jesus to suffer for us, as it is for us to suffer with him. Holy Thursday, Good Friday, and Easter Vigil, the Triduum, our high holy days, lie before us, and we should participate in them to the fullest extent. On Holy Thursday some special features are incorporated into the Mass. The archbishop or the presider washes the feet of twelve parishioners as witnesses to Christ. Baskets of food that we have collected all season for the poor are brought forward to the altar as part of our gifts. Additionally, the Blessed Sacrament is moved to the veiled Adoration chapel for final reverence not to return until Easter.

On Good Friday the congregation venerates the cross, a very moving experience. And then the culmination of our Lenten journey is reached in the dazzling Easter Vigil when the sung *Gloria* is reintroduced, the bells are rung, the holy water fonts are filled with blessed water, and the altar and church are dressed with the most luxurious of God's creations, the lilies. The fast is over, and we have been given the food of eternal life. We gather around the Eucharistic table of fellowship and food, resurrected, and healed for the service of others. Alleluia.

Prayer of the Palms

Accept O Lord the humble palms that greeted you as king as you entered Jerusalem, the week of your passion and death, the same palms that will bless our homes this year. Transform them O Lord, as you transform our bodies with the fires of purification, obtained through prayer, fasting, almsgiving, and sacrifice this Lent. When their ashes are placed on our foreheads, may we be reminded in humility, of our simple origins, that are nothing without your love, and grace, but everything with your mercy. For like the palms we are dust and unto dust we shall return.

PALM SUNDAY: WHAT THEN IS THIS THAT EVEN THE WIND AND THE SEA OBEY? (MARK 4:41) (ALTERNATIVE VERSION)

The baby that was worshipped by the stars, kept warm by the breath of lambs and cattle, and held by Simeon in his uplifted arms, has grown up. One last time while he is alive, the palm trees full of grace bow before him as he makes his triumphal entry into Jerusalem. The next time nature will honor him is when the heavens are rent open in agony as he expires on the cross. It is Palm Sunday and our king has arrived.

Even as a Christian living two thousand years after Jesus' arrival in Jerusalem, we feel the jubilation and expectancy of Palm Sunday. We all clamor for our spring-green palm frond as if our life depended on it, and in a way it does. It is so fresh and malleable, exotic, and luxurious, a sign of hope, life, and abundance, not like the dried yellow sheaf in our homes from last year. It is not recognizable as the precursor of the carbon black ashes of a few weeks ago that we received on our foreheads on Ash Wednesday, reminding us of our humble chemical nature made divine, and yet they are the same. The church is resplendent in red, the color of martyrs, blood, and the spirit. We all know what will happen this week, and yet it doesn't take away from the joy of this day. How could it? He is our sacrificial lamb who will redeem us with his blood. He is our only hope, and we recognize it.

In the synoptic Gospels (Matthew, Mark and Luke's views), Jesus only goes to Jerusalem once for the purpose of the passion and this is it. The entire Gospel has been a pilgrimage by Jesus that begins in Nazareth. Have you been traveling with him by the river, on the mount, in the desert, by the well? It is never too late. Palm Sunday initiates Holy Week, the apex of our liturgical year, culminating in the Triduum, the three feast days of Holy Thursday, Good Friday, and the Easter Vigil. How will you spend them? What will make them different from any other day? Will you have the humility to wash someone's feet, to break bread even with a traitor, to not deny someone his or her identity, to pick up the cross and not complain, or to suffer and die while yet alive?

What good can come from Nazareth they asked? The untorn robe and the split veil of the temple in fulfillment of the Old Testament are proof. We have the benefits of history and hindsight to know the end of the story, but luckily faith is not a gift limited to any historical time. The recent largest study done on religion in the United States claims that membership in institutional religions is down about 10 percent from 86 percent in 1990, to 77 percent in 2001, and in 2008 that percentage is about 71 percent, that is, less Americans believe in the story. Why is that? Is our behavior not believable, our churches failing? Why is the self supreme?

As we welcome him this Palm Sunday, as we take the journey with Christ this week, let us think about how we can make the story of the cross ours as well, so that all will believe it and inherit the gift of eternal life. We know the finale. It is just the beginning of life. We know what good can come from Nazareth!

Christ crucified

HOLY WEEK—THE PASSION, DEATH, AND RESURRECTION: FATHER, INTO YOUR HANDS I COMMEND MY SPIRIT (LUKE 23:46)

At least in the northern hemisphere, during the Lenten season, nature is in her dormant phase. The liturgy parallels the natural world as well, with death and dormancy prevailing, but regardless of geographical location, Lent is a natural and necessary time to think about death.

Death is inevitable. We have been expelled from the Garden of Eden, and along with Jesus, are in the Garden of Gethsemane. In all likelihood we are asking our father to take away our cup, but can we be like Jesus, and accept the father's will? The death of the body will necessarily be physical, but the death of the self, a spiritual abnegation of the will, is more crucial, and in many ways more difficult. Just as the road to the resurrection required the crucifixion and death, the crucifixion necessitated the passion. The passion is that surrendering of self in love for the benefit of others. We can barely stand the things that aggravate us without complaining, how can we endure our necessary passion? The passion of Christ, needed for the sins of all mankind, is vast act of love and unimaginable suffering, even for God.

While physical death may come slowly or suddenly, violently or gently, this death of self is usually a more laborious and languorous task. It can happen in small daily acts of self-dying: acts of forgiveness, sacrifice, reconciliation, humility, and even humiliation, and letting go of expectations which are a function of our own self-will and self-importance. These deaths are befitting in Lent so we will be ready for Easter and all that it signifies. The death of self allows the gates of grace to the Garden of Paradise to open. All these acts of self-dying essentially come down to love.

In Santa Fe, New Mexico, the Archbishop's motto on his coat of arms, *Love One Another Constantly*, sums it all up. It sounds nice, but it is scary when we think of the implications of that mandate. It is a hard task for it doesn't just mean loving the lovable, or those who love us, but loving everyone, and all of the time! Keep it in the forefront of your mind like a road sign giving direction to the recovery of our relationship with God and each other. Unless we can surrender to love, we will not have suffered our own passion in our own Garden of Gethsemane. We will be given the strength to self-die if we ask the father to make way for the paradise.

It is Holy Week, the most sacred week of the year. Will you make it different from every other week in some respect? Take the time to attend the various liturgies that only occur this week. They can be spiritual necessities that will assist in self-dying. On Easter, dormant branches and bulbs will assume their full nature. Annual and perennial flowers proclaim spring; life from the frozen cathedral of nature emerges. Watch a tree come back to life from the icy desert; make acts of self-giving for life is eternal. We are no longer wandering refugees; the winter is over. The splendor, suffering, and death in the sojourn of life are given meaning. Love reigns, and death is overcome by uniting ourselves with the passion, death, and resurrection of our Redeemer, Jesus Christ.

EASTER: HE RAISES THE NEEDY FROM THE DUST (1 SAM 2:8)

Culturally, even as a Christian nation where Christians celebrate Christmas, why don't we celebrate Easter as visibly? Is it because Easter is viewed as less marketable, more internal, and personal, or even not viewed as important? We may get new clothes, Easter baskets, and candy for the kids, conduct Easter egg hunts, or go out to brunch. Are we searching for something right in front of us like the eggs in the rectory garden, the living room, or the refrigerator?

It is Holy Week, the most sacred week of the year. Can you make time to attend the various liturgies that only occur at this time of year? Think of it as spa experience for the soul, nourishing, and cleansing, a spiritual necessity. The ashes of Lent have been washed away. Did Lent make a difference to you?

This week begins on Palm Sunday. That jubilant day, Jesus enters Jerusalem, recognized with the semblance of a humble king. Did his disciples ever think he would be crucified before the week is over, or that most of them would be martyred too for this man they followed? We may celebrate that day with an ecumenical blessing of palms followed by a procession to the church, or accepting our frond at Mass. A reconciliation service prepares us for the holy days, a Seder meal, or a potluck of our favorite meat free foods mirrors in cultural ways the Holy Thursday supper.

Holy Thursday starts with Morning Prayer and ends with evening Mass of the Lord's Supper and Eucharistic adoration. The Blessed Sacrament chapel only looks like this once a year, a veritable garden of veiled lilies foreshadowing the resurrection, as we see Jesus for the last time before the crucifixion at the altar of repose in the chapel. On Good Friday there can be a passion play of the Stations of the Cross, following veneration of the cross, and a communion service. Saturday Morning prayer precedes the Easter Vigil, that evening when the catechumens are baptized, and the candidates are received into full communion with the church. And then Easter Sunday, the blessing of the Easter baskets, and infant baptisms. The life of spring from the frozen posture of death and nature is reclaimed. The icy world explodes into life. We are no longer without hope, the merging of human and divine wills through love, as Thomas Merton would say. The winter is over; suffering is made meaningful and complete through the resurrection of Our Lord Jesus Christ. It is an eschatological reality—a reality now in the passing world and a promise in the fulfillment of time. Blessed Easter to all+

6

Special Supplement for Lent and Easter I

Francis for Lent

Basilica of St. Francis of Assisi, Italy

AN OVERVIEW

He is the patron saint of many parishes and probably the most beloved saint in the world. We know lots of little things about him: the birds and animals loved him, he was kind, he wore a brown tunic, and he was poor. He lived in Assisi. We may even have had the privilege of traveling to Assisi, of being in that quaint medieval town, of walking its cobblestone streets as the sun sets, and the light in the sky is indescribable, the clouds part over his basilica, and despite the throngs of visitors there is an audible hush. It is so peaceful. Giotto di Bondone's art continues from the Vatican, to Padua, to Assisi, to depict in the massive church the milestones, some of which are mythical but symbolic, of St. Francis' life. Like St. Peter's Basilica his is filled with people from all over the world humbled to see the place where the remains of Francis repose under the altar.

We probably know other small facts about him. Some of us may know more than others, especially religious and lay members of his order, scholars, and authors. But if Francis continues to capture our imagination eight hundred years after his death, what is it about him that really has set the world afire as it has since his time in the life of the Catholic Church, and even in other faiths? Was it his torn, bare feet, his worn tunic, his willingness to beg for bread, or sleep in the cold. Or was it the common denominator of all these particulars—that he saw the church as the expression of Gospel values, and that he believed Gospel values were to be lived? Through his willingness to literally live the Gospel he received the great love that Jesus had for him that would rekindle God's message of love. No one before or since has been like him such is the uniqueness of each individual. If we can even catch a glimpse of his message this season we will be changed at a very fundamental level. This Lent, not as scholars, but as simple people, let us follow Francis and become reacquainted with his story, and his meaning in our lives, for while times change, his story is an expression of God's eternal love.

ASH WEDNESDAY AND ALMSGIVING

Giovanni di Pietro di Bernardone, whom we know as Francis, was born in feudal Italy in 1181 or 1182. His father, who had spent considerable time in France, called his son Francesco. Francis was actually named after St. John the Baptist, whom we became more acquainted with in

Advent, and that appellation was not a misnomer. He was a lot like John in John's fundamental message that "He must increase, but I must decrease." Francis was not like other saints whom we know for their holy childhoods like St. Therese of Lisieux or St. Rose of Lima. His youthful years were marked by delight in nature, then mirth and valor as he aspired to be a knight. He was energetic, and engaging, but not immune to the suffering and the poverty he saw around him. A period of torturous imprisonment, as part of the horrors of medieval war changed him, when in prison he found a small Bible in his own language. Upon his release from captivity he could no longer see the world in the same way, and could only think about uniting himself to the goodness of Jesus.

This week Ash Wednesday and the start of the Lenten season arrive. What can we learn from Francis this Lent? One his first acts marking his gradual conversion to the Gospel way of life was to give away his clothes. He later asked for them back, but the significance of that initial renunciation set in, and he did it again, this time giving his father back the clothes he had been provided with as a son. His father then rejected him, and in that denouncement Francis recognized the significance of the authentic love of God the father as the one true relationship defining behavior. The embrace of this concept becomes the canopy of his worldview of how we should be in the world. Surely we have plenty of clothes, shoes, and blankets we could give to the poor. Let us begin this Lent with almsgiving. As you fall into the envelope of sleep in your comfortable bed or in a the poverty of a homeless shelter, say the *Our Father* slowly over and over as if learning it for the first time, and wake up praying it as well. Start this Lent like Francis with the recognition of the principles expressed in this perfect prayer. It will steer us through the Lenten journey as it did Francis' life of service to the realization of the kingdom.

THE FIRST SUNDAY OF LENT—SUSPENSION AND SURRENDER

Illness has many facets—it is personal, familial, social, and spiritual. Illness is not just difficult for the one who suffers it but for those who share in it as well. Think of a family member with a constant asthmatic cough, a child crying from flu symptoms that are mysterious to him, or an older patient whose arthritic pains limit her mobility and flexibility such that simple tasks like dressing or feeding herself are impossible. As family members or even as healthcare workers we may be uncomfortable being around ill people because we feel helpless, are aggravated by such symptoms, or because illness is disquieting to us. As holy as he was Francis was not exempt from the illness of his deprived body, and depression over his perceived failures, in fact, he claimed suffering came from God, and united us with him when we offered it back to him. God is close to us in pain and illness. That thought might be what gives us the strength to endure.

Historically and biblically it has always been difficult to be around lepers. Great saints like recently canonized St. Damien of Moloka'i and St. Francis of Assisi recognized the social and spiritual rejection of lepers, and made their reconciliation with them by living amongst the lepers and loving them. The lepers who lived outside of the city walls repulsed Francis; they were his greatest fear. But when he literally embraced a leper, instead of retreating, he found that the only real fear was in his mind. That embrace liberated him from the cultural paradigm that ostracized the lepers, and enveloped Francis like a halo in Christ's commandment to love one another. This event suspended him from the limitations of the mind, and connected him to the joyful message and the magnanimousness of the love of our God of the Gospel.

Interestingly, another way Francis continued to create the Gospel reality was by calling all he met including the animals and nature "brother" or "sister," and greeting all with peace as he met, and departed from them. This use of inclusive and positive language created that reality, much like the words "thank you" and "you're welcome" or other ways we say things kindly that create our reality. The body in all its infirmities was his brother, and death his sister. Can we see the truth and comfort in this when we are ill or lose a loved one?

A major societal problem we have is that of homelessness. Homelessness is all around us, and we can make a difference by caring for the homeless. There are many homeless shelters you can assist in as a volunteer to help by providing clothes, prepared meals, paying for milk or helping with work in the shelter. We need not be repulsed by homelessness. Not all the homeless can be accommodated in shelters, and in the day you will see them at street intersections, in parking lots, at work and yes, even in our churches. Some say they have to leave Mass early to get checked into the shelter for a meal and a night of sleep in a sleeping bag on the floor. We can avert our eyes, make believe they aren't there, make judgments that they need to work or aren't like us but these are the thoughts and behaviors of the cultural illusion of entitlement, the mythic beliefs that we have all learned that you get what you deserve.

Listen to the story of the Gospel through Francis. It resonates with the beating of our own heart, capturing our faith and imagination in a new world of equity. When we embrace that concept, a homeless person or the people we view as lepers in our lives change. Don't let this opportunity pass you by in Lent and everyday. Sleep and food and kindness are basic human needs that Francis realized need to be met. Poverty is the biggest societal illness, and the task of all to heal; it makes us uncomfortable only if we don't embrace it. We are all lepers and if we can embrace each other, we will be embraced. Lent is a good time to learn the surrender, and joyfulness of Francis.

THE SECOND SUNDAY IN LENT—THE INCARNATION AND FASTING

"I have to confess to you and God that during this Lent I have eaten cakes made with lard." Such was St. Francis' simplicity, innocence, example, and purity of heart over the food he begged for, and was grateful to have eaten. Such poverty of spirit and body was the benchmark of Francis' humble life and that of his followers to come. No coin was ever to be accepted, no reserve of goods or money to be accrued, only what was begged for on a daily basis. Beggars can't be choosers they say but are they different from us? Not many of us could live on what we asked for daily, and yet one out of six people in the world is hungry. Is that a stunning fact we just read and then go out to eat, ignoring or not acting on God in each other? Francis fed the animals from the birds to the wolf, to the half frozen, starving bees that crawled to him as they died when he offered them their own honey with wine. It is such an image of love and compassion! His peaceful message of harmony with all creation matched his joyful poverty.

Francis was absorbed in the Incarnation, the changing of history forever when the son of God came into the world. While plays had been staged, and art drawn depicting the nativity of Jesus, imagine the actual reenactment of the nativity staged by Francis! While the animals looked on, it is said that as Francis held the infant, the actual Christ child appeared in his arms and the animals worshipped. Such was the union of God with Francis.

In Lent we traditionally abstain from meat on Friday or from our favorite foods or drinks in sacrifice for Christ's passion, and fast from meals as further sacrifice. While these can be very valuable and meaningful practices, have we ever felt the pangs of fasting and abstinence to the level that Francis undoubtedly did in his austere life? Our penance in this form of sacrifice would not manifest as a doom and gloom, sackcloth and ashes attitude but one of joy for the reign of God is here! Francis recognized that true penance is characterized by a change of heart in which we open ourselves to love no matter where it comes from or who needs it. His worn, rough tunic concealed a cloak of wonder for God is everywhere, in everyone, in everything. The universe can only contain him in its infinity, and in our emptiness, through fasting from anything we enjoy, we can allow that infinity to fill us.

Spring may be coming but the earth is still bare, perhaps our souls a mirror of that emptiness. Sometimes we have to give up everything in order for God to come in. St. Francis understood his namesake St. John the Baptist and his realization that "He must increase but I must decrease." As we lose things—a parent dying, missing Mass due to illness, obligation or circumstance, a decline of health or status—if we can stay calm, and think of this scripture, God does fill us. We can stop the struggle, be in the moment and know there is nothing to be afraid of. He will fill us, and we will no longer have to be our limited selves.

In the next five weeks of Lent can we be enthusiastically generous, frolicking in the joy of giving what we have of ourselves at home, at work, in church, and in our community? We have been through Advent and the Christmas season just a short while ago. Do we understand the significance of the Incarnation yet? God is here! We may not be ordained or Third Order Franciscans but we can be Franciscans at heart by wearing the robe of practicality, frugality, and charity through our joyful, meaningful, personal fasting and abstinence. Distinguish what you need from what you want, and then give that up too. Can we as Francis see poverty as a privilege, trust that God will provide even in the barren months of winter, joblessness, homelessness and worry?

Look at the birds in their brown habits cavorting in the snow, tapping the earth for hidden seeds. Buy a birdhouse and tenderly offer the birds food as we participate in establishing the reign of God. Watch as subtle green and encased buds slowly appear on the dormant trees. Light a votive candle in the church, in your home, in your soul, a small hopeful dancing flame of life. Begin the spring-cleaning of the soul by fasting from what isn't important. You'll be surprised how much isn't needed and what it will be replaced with.

THE THIRD SUNDAY IN LENT—REBUILD MY HOUSE

As Catholics we probably are somewhat familiar with the mandate to Francis from Jesus as his voice spoke from the cross at San Damiano saying to Francis, "Rebuild my Church." Francis of course interpreted this to mean to repair the dilapidated, abandoned church that had fallen into ruin through neglect. No doubt that was an aspect of this message; the house of God should not be in disrepair. Later Pope Innocent III, the channel through whom Francis had requested to establish his order, had a dream in which Francis was holding up St. John Lateran Basilica, the Pope as the Bishop of Rome's church. Innocent accurately recognized the symbolic value of this dream. Innocent saw the purity of Francis' understanding of the Gospel and allowed him to establish his mendicant order to preach as an order of the church. He understood that the love Francis exemplified was the building block of what it means to be a church, a Christian, and to follow Christ. Without that love, the church is just an empty ruin. When they embraced it was a mutual embrace as holy and as genuine as the one Francis gave to the leper.

Today we too know that that church was more than the mud and stonewalls of San Damiano and the other churches Francis went on to restore. Certainly making a special place fitting for the reservation of the Blessed Sacrament, a house of prayer not unlike where Jesus prayed, and a place of worship is appropriate. Even Francis at the time thought the physical rebuilding of the structure of the church was his calling but it was just the beginning of the meaning of his work. As he delved deeper into the meaning of poverty, which is our total reliance on God, his concept like ours grew, just as we are growing from going to church to being the church. Indeed, that bigger institution of the church composed of humans, would intrinsically have it share of successes and failures. That church is even more than the Catholic Church but the very building blocks of society, our relationships with each other, and all nations and faiths. Despite his heritage as a rich son of a merchant, Francis knew he was a son of God, and that all men were his brothers. Pressured by his followers to establish a rule by which they all might practically live, Francis was dumbfounded, for to him the only rule was the Gospel of love that repaired social and natural relationships. Revenue and comfort were not the things he was concerned about. But as he was dying at the age of young age of forty-four, Francis did make some specifications about how the order would live which he dictated in his *Testament,* and left behind to comfort his brothers.

As Francis was dying and the donkey wept, he said. "I have done my part, may Christ teach you to do yours." What is our part? Is it to help clean and decorate the church as part of the Altar Society? Is it to replace or restore parts of the church in need of care and paid for through the Friends of the Cathedral or the generosity of private donors? Is it to help the poor through the Peace and Social Justice Committee or the St. Vincent DePaul Society? Is it to glorify God in sung prayer led by the choir, to promote sociability and community through coffee and donuts with the Donut Committee? Yes, it is all of these things and more, but it is also the church of our soul, carved out in our very being by God before conception in our mother's womb. It is more than a one-time event but a lifestyle of baptismal immersion in God. We are the frame of the church. He is our DNA.

Lent is almost halfway over; we are in the wilderness of winter. Spring and new life are on the horizon. We are at an intersection, learning through Francis that all is impermanent except the eternal love of God. Living in the world with love will we answer the call, "Rebuild my Church," as Francis did? This is not a quiz but a challenge. What will you do to mend the broken relationships and friendships of people, and the devastation of our planet, both torn asunder by the self-importance of sin and made an empty church?

THE FOURTH SUNDAY IN LENT—CHIARA, MARY, AND CREATION

No understanding of Francis would be complete without considering the special relationship between St. Francis and St. Clare (Chiara). Clare was not just the female equivalent or contemporary of St. Francis, but like each one of us, a special person with unique gifts from God, invited to respond to the ardent message of Francis on the importance of love, poverty, and peace. Forfeiting her inheritance and status in feudal Assisi, she left her home under the cover of night to be sequestered in the monastery of St. Paul as she transitioned to this new way of living. Shorn of her beautiful hair she clung to the altar at the monastery of St. Paul when her relatives tried to bring her back to her paternal home, but it was not to be for she had received her calling. She followed Francis' teachings and behavior, and resided cloistered, in the church of San Damiano, until the end of her life with the women who would then follow her.

The obvious love between Francis and Clare was very real, but not in a romantic or sexual way, although this is the love that most of us as laity share in marriage, and that is good. Nor was it an unrequited "Romeo and Juliet" type of love. Rather, their love was transcendent, an intimate, naked, honest love where they could fully be themselves, radiant with the object of their mutual love of Jesus Christ. Clare adhered as strictly to Francis' rule of poverty as he did, and in some sense more so as she was to outlive him by twenty-seven years. The pure Clare served as the spiritual advisor to the friars after the death of Francis, and as the head of the Poor Clares, an order that lives on to this day.

Francis likewise loved our Blessed Mother Mary, particularly in her role as the Mother of God, someone human who allowed the divine word to physically become flesh. She fulfilled the role God asked of her, a role that changed history and made it possible for us to be reconciled to God. Can we say that about ourselves, that what we do makes a difference for the reign of God by allowing God to work through us? Can Mary our mother help us know what it is we are meant to do and how to do it?

In 1225, Francis, essentially blind from years of physical deprivation and illness, dictated his famed *Canticle of the Creatures* in which he immortalized the sun that he saw as our brother, the moon as our sister, earth and sky, and fire and water. Creation was good, complementary, not polarized but reconciled in a relationship of harmony and peace. Nature, creation, was necessary for our well-being and redemption.

This Sunday is *Laetare* Sunday, the Sunday of rejoicing for Lent. Half of Lent has passed. Hope is on the horizon. One of the chief descriptions that we find of Francis in biographies, his prayers, and the art of many, was his ability to find joy in the moment and in creation. Can we find joy today in the beauty of the natural world that we are stewards to? Read the *Canticle of the Creatures*. Take a walk, or sit outside and experience it. Or, if the weather is inclement, spend sometime looking outside. Talk to the birds; give them some bread or seeds today. Think about Clare, Mary, and the sun, the moon, air, sky, earth, and the chastity of water and praise them. Can you see—they, like us, are the all of the same essence, the container of God!

THE FIFTH SUNDAY IN LENT—ISLAM, MAY THE LORD GIVE YOU PEACE

While we know many of the events of Francis' life, one we may be less familiar with is the central relationship of St. Francis with the Sultan of Egypt, Malik al-Kamil. In the time of Francis, the Fifth Crusade, a "holy war," was being waged for possession of the Holy Land against the Muslims who were viewed as enemies and infidels. This war raged for many years, and tens of thousands of soldiers in the Crusades, the enemy, and innocent men, women, and children were mutilated and murdered in the most brutal of ways.

After Francis' death, art, literature and biographies of Francis were controlled and revised, destroyed and filtered to meet the needs of papal politics so this is a chapter in Francis' life that has somewhat been misunderstood and underestimated. The artist Giotto had Francis walking through fire to prove to the sultan that his was the real God, but the real God does not need drama, legend, or embellishment. Francis met face to face with the sultan in a loving and respectful manner, with the equality of love that began and ended with Francis' standard greeting, "May the Lord give you peace."

Francis, who had experienced the trauma of war personally, and was deeply devoted to the Gospel life, knew that true peace is above sociopolitical, economic or religious boundaries, and he was fervent in extending this message to popes and sultans. He journeyed to Egypt in the hopes of negotiating a peace treaty, which he did achieve, only to be rejected by the church because the Muslims, like most perceived enemies, were the lepers and the wolves. Francis was not a scholar, and he shied away from academics in favor of understanding that the most important written word was love in the story of the Gospel made man in Jesus Christ. His two most quoted verses of scripture, which he purposely honed in on, were "to love thy enemy" and "blessed are the peacemakers." The Gospel to Francis was meant to be taken literally.

Some say Francis so desired to be like Christ that he went to Egypt to be martyred, but this is antithetical to Francis' mission of promoting reconciliation and building the church. There is a difference between wanting to be martyred and being willing, and that was the case for Francis, such was the depth of his understanding of "Build my Church." His approach was not that of eradicating enemies or forcing conversion, but promoting peace through the non-violence of love and the message of Christ. In this sense he was and we can be martyrs.

The peace that Francis negotiated with the Muslim leader was rejected because of our failure to embrace the "leper" and the literalness of the Gospel. We chose friction, self-centeredness, and unforgiveness over God's plan. If the peace achieved eight hundred years ago with Francis and Malik al-Kamil over the sites of the Holy Land had been accepted and maintained, the world would be much different than it is now.

Francis was not a religious extremist or a hippy flower child but a man like all humans, marred by war but blessed with the mark of faith, a man who realized that the peace that comes from God is the only true form of peace and it is called love. Are we willing to work for peace this Lent? Its starts with forgiveness. Let us forgive each other again and again and pursue the holy work of peace in our lifetime.

THE SIXTH SUNDAY IN LENT—PALM SUNDAY AND THE STIGMATA

In the movie, *Francis and Clare*, one of the most beautiful moments ever captured on film is there for us to behold. It is Christmas Eve and St. Francis is reenacting the nativity scene for the first time in a neighboring city. Clare is ill in bed and unable to attend. She hears a child crying, forces herself to get up, and makes her way to the small chapel at San Damiano where she lives with the sisters. There the crucified Christ comes down from the cross and becomes a baby in her arms. Her mother, sister, and the other Poor Clares hear the crying too and come to the chapel to witness this miraculous event, and fall to their knees in adoration. Clare is beaming with maternal, ecstatic love. It is a scene true or fabled that captures the meeting of the Incarnation—Christ, our Savior as a beautiful baby came to us and will die out of love for us. The cross ultimately is a vision of that love and that is what we need to know to understand the purpose of life and to bear our own personal sufferings.

While Francis was more interested in the Incarnation than other mysteries, and felt the joy from God's advent into the world that saved us, he certainly understood the need for the passion in Jesus' and our own lives. Francis, entrepreneur, soldier, and follower of Christ, pursued that love to the point that he became the first person to receive the stigmata, the five wounds of Christ's passion, on his own body. Some say the stigmata came from an angel who delivered it to him, others that the burning, internal love of God made its way to the outside of his flesh, still others that Jesus himself gave the wounds to Francis. No matter where they came from the significance of the stigmata was that it allowed Francis to participate in everything Jesus experienced. While they were certainly a mark of God's favor with him they were still painful, and marks Francis felt unworthy to bear, yet he did in silence as he tried to keep the wounds hidden and not bring them to anyone's attention.

Imagine seeing these wounds on yourself. Most of us won't receive the stigmata of Jesus yet we have our own wounds. It is our purpose to share and bind each other's wounds that are part and parcel of the human story and just as surely we will share in his resurrection. While about three hundred other saints (mostly women) have receive the stigmata since that time, we all have a mark that unites us to him forever if we let it consume us as Francis did. It is not just a mark for our catechumens this Lent but ours too—the union of brother fire of the spirit with sister water in the indelible water of Baptism.

Appropriately Francis received the stigmata on the Feast of the Exaltation of the Holy Cross towards the end of the liturgical year, and two years before he died as he was meditating at the mountainous La Verna. There he also composed *The Praises of God* for his brothers to remind them of the glory of God. In Lent, like Jesus in the desert and at Gethsemane, and Francis at La Verna, let us model ourselves after them and pray, *The Praises of God* with the fire of Francis:

> *You are the Holy Lord who does wonderful things. You are strong. You are great. You are the most high. You are the almighty king. You holy father, King of heaven and earth. You are three and one, the Lord God of gods; You are the good, all good, the highest good. Lord God living and true. You are love, charity; You are wisdom, You are humility, You are patience, You are beauty, You are meekness, You are security, You are rest, You are gladness and joy, You are our hope, You are justice, You are moderation, You are all our riches to sufficiency. You are beauty, You are meekness, You are the protector, You are our custodian and defender, You are strength, You are refreshment, You are our hope, You are our faith, You are our charity, You are all our sweetness, You are our eternal life; great and wonderful Lord, almighty God, Merciful Savior.*

EASTER AND THE GOSPEL—AND IT IS IN DYING THAT WE ARE BORN TO ETERNAL LIFE

Francis took two small loaves of bread and some water with him on his forty day fast in the desert and only ate half of the loaf. Our forty days of Lent are over too. What did we do? Did we give alms, fast, abstain, pray, forgive, promote peace, and be joyful? Easter is what these practices have been leading up to.

Christ has risen. The resurrection of Christ promises us that new, eternal life as well if we love one another. Life is not static but changing and now it has the new dimension of the resurrection. Did we change over Lent as we learned about Francis? Do we understand the supreme value of all life, the lepers, enemies and Muslims of our time? Did we see a leper, someone we don't like or one who treats us unjustly and still reach out and love them? Did we feed a wolf or rescue an abused animal that had to fight for its life because no one would help it? Did we love close by or afar a "Muslim" who loves their loving God? Did we study Francis to observe the holy Gospel of Our Lord Jesus Christ through the example of St. Francis of Assisi? Did we promote Gospel justice that is measured by love, and ecological justice that is promoted by care of the earth? Did we tend our gardens and our souls so that new life could spring from them? Do we have the superabundant fertility of hope that Francis brought us in his Gospel-lived life?

Who is Francis? In medieval times Francis was a unique person; not since Jesus was anyone like him, yet this can be said of us as well. Francis was like Christ in all ways and that is how we need to be too. That sounds nice but it means we need to give up ourselves to do that and do we really want to give up the pride of our precious personal identity? Francis understood the significance of the resurrection and so he could live for others in a free, poor, joyful way. Francis is not just for Lent, for like Jesus Christ, he is for all time.

Christmas made the word become flesh. What does this mean? The word of God, his Gospel message of love, is real, and fulfilled in the person of Christ now through the gift of the resurrection to us. Today in historical time we have to "personify" that love. Easter takes us from the limitations of the solely human form to the eternal life of the body and the spirit that has lived in us since God conceived of us before we were conceived in our mother's womb. Resurrection is a reality today. What does that mean to you? This may seem like a lot of questions at the conclusion of the Lenten season and of a series on Francis, but there is only one answer. Easter is not the finale nor should prayer, fasting, or almsgiving end. The holy season of Lent and the Triduum are seasons of love—messy, intimate, naked, and beautiful periods in our lives. They need to be part of our lived faith.

In Francis' and other periods, the lepers had to wear a bell around their neck, announcing their presence so others could retreat. The Easter bells of the church are ringing like leper bells chiming, "Francis, Francis!" As his brothers and sisters we are his authentic relatives. With Christ as our Savior and Francis as our guide let us continue his spirit into the Easter season and beyond into Ordinary Time. As the bells sound will we run from or towards the leper? It is up to us. There is no reason to be sad or nostalgic about the passing of Francis or Jesus. The promise of hope, the pledge of eternal life is possible through the supreme human and divine inclination of love. With the resurrection we are the new Francis for our time.

7

Special Supplement for Lent and Easter II

Learning Mark by Heart in Lent

Crown of thorns with preserved roses

WEEK 1 ASH WEDNESDAY

THE FOUR GOSPELS OF the New Testament canon, the story of the entry of God into relationship with humanity through his son Jesus Christ, is the story of the arrival of the kingdom of God in a passing world. This good news of salvation through Jesus Christ incarnate is the heart of each of the four Gospels. While this fundamental and profound message remains the same, each Gospel is unique in its author, audience, writing style, and stories, for each historical era makes its own demands on God's people. This differentiation enhances and augments their cumulative presentation of God's gift to us, his beloved Son. This liturgical year, Year B, we learn about Jesus through the eyes and understandings of the first evangelist, St. Mark. His is a story with a dual theme—that of learning about the life, death, and resurrection of Jesus, and then, how to be as Jesus was.

In this new literary genre created by Mark, the narrative story termed by him "Gospel" means "good news." Chronologically, experts surmise Mark's was the first Gospel account, written by an anonymous John Mark of first century Rome, sometime between 60 to 70 CE, although exact dates cannot be determined. His work may have been composed shortly before or after the destruction of the Jerusalem Temple in 70 CE. This was a fragile and tense time of intense persecution of the first Christians under the rule of the Emperor Nero. These early Christians and those who were uncommitted but interested in the good news were the recipients of Mark's urgent message. Many of them were thrown into the Roman Coliseum and were viciously slaughtered because of their faith as entertainment, along with entire species of animals. Others were reduced to ashes and burned alive at night as torches to illuminate the streets. Although the oral traditions had kept the story of Jesus alive, and the end of the story was known, Mark's Gospel was brilliantly written as a breathtaking apocalyptic account wherein the identity of Jesus is gradually revealed through nature, demons, and disciples, and finally through his death and resurrection.

The Gospel of Mark is a short, sacred story of sacrifice, discipleship, suffering, and the kingdom that has begun now and will be fully realized in the future, made possible by the gratuitous love of the father, son and Holy Spirit. It is a perfect Gospel to read and study in Lent, for to know Jesus means to follow him to the cross, and isn't that what Lent is about? Through the prism of Mark, in this beautiful and vivid

Christological mystery story, we learn who the enigmatic Jesus was and what it means to be involved with him today as a disciple in life and ministry. Announced through his preaching and made possible to all who believe in him, in his words and deeds, Jesus invites us to respond to the offer of relationship with him and the father through the spirit. The incredulity of this invitation to the kingdom of God is not that we would draw near to God but that God would draw near to us in a relationship of love as we saw repeatedly in the Old Testament. Like the post-Easter Christian community, we are challenged to go beyond membership in the church to discipleship, to transform our lives and ministry using the Gospel portrait of Jesus. As we come forward to receive the mark of our faith on Ash Wednesday, let us be willing to grow further in faith through the active service of discipleship this Lent.

WEEK 2 JOHN AND DEMONS

Just like the anticipation we feel at a play when the curtain rises, so too does the dramatic Gospel account of Mark begin with the curtain of his theater pulled apart—the heavens are torn open to reveal the story of Jesus Christ as son of God and servant, suffering, and resurrected Messiah. Unlike the Gospel of Luke, the only account that begins with the story of the nativity, Mark begins his mystery Gospel at the beginning of Jesus' public life—the beautiful scene at the Jordan River where his cousin John the Baptist baptizes Jesus. We get no clue that they knew each other as cousins, only that John realized that the man who approached him for Baptism by water was the "stronger one." God's voice emerges from the clouds confirming Jesus as his beloved son in whom he is well pleased, and his Holy Spirit descends upon Jesus. Before we have too much time to think about what the spirit is, Jesus retreats to the desert for forty days to be tended by wild animals and angels and tempted by Satan. What a stunning image of reconciliation between heaven and earth, he, their maker, is cared for by their reciprocal love and service!

After this time of announcement and preparation, Jesus, with apparent and undeniable authority, recruits his apostles. He is so compelling that the apostles respond intensely and immediately. Committedly they follow him through a series of powerful physical healings, indeed miracles, as proof of his identity. The people are repeatedly amazed; a proper and colloquial reaction to his miracles, and even the demons that he drove out recognized his true identity. It will take some time for people of his own nature to do so, and Jesus is in no rush for he does not want his nature to be misunderstood. "Who is this man that even the wind and the sea obey?" Nature, his creation, knew him, so do our demons. Do we?

The drama of Mark's Gospel centers round what he calls the messianic secret. What this means is that his entire Gospel is dedicated to the disclosure of Jesus as Messiah, one in their midst whom they did not recognize until the centurion's confession at the end of the Gospel where he dramatically declares that truly this man was the son of God. Jesus keeps his identity a secret so there are no false expectations of his messiahship. This Lent we have the same opportunity to see the power of Jesus in his words and deeds. It is not enough to say we believe in him—we must also act out that belief. Take some time to sit down today and read his words in the shortest Gospel, that of Mark, to become acquainted first hand with Jesus' deeds in this powerful narrative. Think—what do I believe about Jesus? How can I practically live out that belief? This is our challenge for all times as Christians.

Shortly after the inauguration of Jesus' public ministry we learn that John the Baptist is beheaded, foreshadowing the death of Jesus and the apostles as harbingers of the word as John was. St. Mark was martyred and beheaded too in Egypt by the Muslims, his body then surreptitiously smuggled into Venice, Italy under a slab of mutton that the Muslims would not touch. We will not be burned as lampposts as in ancient Rome to prove our belief in the Messiah, but like the beheaded John and Mark, we need to loose our heads over him and put on the mind of Christ. We have Lent to learn again, to reconvert, to the costly and joyous commitment to follow Jesus, as we all must to the cross that leads to everlasting life.

WEEK 3 HEALING AND BLINDNESS

When we read the Gospels, there seem to be an awful lot of sick people in those stories. They are blind, have leprosy (in Mark's time leprosy included other skin disorders like eczema), yet we still may wonder, is this Gospel relevant to us? Are we blind, are we lepers, are we deaf, and do we hemorrhage? But the answer to these questions, and the pertinence of Mark's Gospel ring true even if we are not ill. While illness is not a punishment for individual sin, it is a product of corporate sin as a race.

Whether we suffer a discrete, named disease or not, we are all ill in the sense that we are imperfect and not reconciled to the wholeness of God's' plan.

As proof that the kingdom of God is at hand, when Jesus cures the ill, he first forgives the relative intangibility of sin. On the road to Bethsaida, Jesus attempts a lesson in discipleship, explaining to his disciples that he must die, but that he will be resurrected. Then they meet an unnamed blind man who is brought to him. With his spittle Jesus gradually heals the man in stages. The man's returning vision is at first blurred and then complete. The man was asked by Jesus not to go into the village, for the time for disclosure of Jesus' identity had not yet come.

In the second half of Mark's Gospel, on the road to Jerusalem outside of Jericho, Jesus and his disciples encounter the blind beggar Bartimaeus sitting by the side of the road. Bartimaeus cries out for mercy, and beseeches Jesus as Son of David to cure him while others rebuked him. Jesus invited an act of faith by asking Bartimaeus what he would like him to do and the blind man said he wanted to see. Bartimaeus' faith in Jesus allowed his sight to be completely healed and the disciples' eyes were opened too, allowing them into the realm of faith. This is the first time other than with Peter and the demons that a human recognizes Jesus as Messiah and the title, Son of David, is introduced. These two blind stories enhance and bracket each other on the journey that divulges Jesus' identity and mission in Jerusalem. Sight, signifying faith, goes from being blind, to blurry, to the fullness of vision that includes suffering. These healing accounts are not just about blindness and slowly returning sight and curing, but have the Christological function of revealing who Jesus is, and the role of faith in healing.

As in Mark's healing of the first blind man at Bethsaida, we are gradually healed in stages to see the reality of who he is. Going through Lent over and over again, getting up every morning, indeed every minute, is our opportunity to be healed in stages, to resolve the elusive shapes and blindness of sin to see Jesus like the brilliance of the dawn, the light of the setting sun, or the moonlight of his face. We will always have the sick with us. Indeed we may become one of them. Sickness, healing, and death are integral parts of the experiences of life, as fundamental as joy, sorrow, and all the emotions and events that we have been given to experience. Faith is our only true medicine.

As Mark shows us, there is a transformative nature of illness. The needs of others are the doors of insight into ourselves. While illness may not change, it can be a vantage point, a place of fluidity, transformation, conversion, and transcendence because we are on the border between what is known and unknown, life and death, and sickness and health. Illness is an occasion to mend our fragmentation, our fundamental brokenness, and estrangement from the original intent of happiness with God, and to convert to wholeness and seeing. The inner core of Lent and healing is conversion. Healing is a new way to see and believe. Jesus is the compassionate healer and more. Heal us as only you can O Lord!

WEEK 4 PETER

Scholars describe the Gospel of Mark historically as a Petrine story, that is, it is an account by Peter to Mark, his associate, like Luke was Paul's associate. If you have had a chance to read the first few chapters so far, Mark's lively style should be apparent, not just to expediently convey the Good News but because the Parousia, or second coming of Christ was expected soon.

In Mark, Peter is a central figure in the cast of characters, serving as the foil to help reveal Jesus' identity, the Messianic secret, when Jesus has taught through word and deed what he came to do. Peter is the first to be called as a disciple. He walks away from his lucrative career as a fisherman never thinking he will become the foremost fisher of men. Yet Peter, flawed and gifted, has a hard time understanding what Jesus is up to. Protectively and ignorantly, Peter tells Jesus that he does not need to go to Jerusalem to meet his fate. Jesus goes so far to respond to Peter, "Get behind me Satan." These are strong condemning words to the first of apostles, but Jesus must correct the misinterpretation of his messiahship. Peter wants to negotiate and we are a lot like him. Don't we do that too in prayer, bargaining for the easier way out? Do we have to go to Jerusalem? Do we have to undergo Calvary? Do we have to take up the cross? Surely this was not meant for me?

Mark's Gospel gradually builds up to reveal who Jesus is as his perception by others evolved from Jewish teacher and healer of unparalleled authority, to Messiah, to the son of David and then son of God. As we are learning, Mark's whole Gospel was written to gradually reveal the mystery of the hidden kingdom of God as embodied in Jesus, and breaking into life in the present. The mystery is that he is not only the Messiah but also what kind of Messiah he is. He is not the one expected in the Old Testament to reestablish the throne of David as a physical, political, prosperous one, but a *suffering* Messiah, *servant* and *son of God*. Jesus asks Peter, "Who do people say that I am?" and Peter responds that some say he is Elijah, or John the Baptist or a prophet. Then Jesus asks, "Who do you say that I am? Peter responds, "You are the Christ."

The throngs of crowds build up, and those who at first followed him everywhere, abate. Admiration of Jesus changes to envy, amazement to hostility, and enthusiasm to rejection. Even Peter denies Christ three times as Jesus foretold. Jesus takes Peter, James, and John with him up to the mountain top where they see the transfiguration of Jesus in his resurrected and eternal form, as one of his final acts before going to his destiny in Jerusalem. We hear again the voice of the father beholding his beloved son. Yet they still misinterpret who he is. Following Christ is costly. Do we understand any better the gift of the kingdom of God?

Who do we say that he is? Are we willing to go all the way to Jerusalem and beyond to Easter morning? Can we use conflict, pain, suffering, and death in our lives to grow, indeed to blossom with new life? Peter the rock failed but the church is built upon his recommitted blunders of faith. Without failure there is no story. God always precedes us; so, let us follow in discipleship, prayer, and service as the last of servants. This is what Lent means. Can you see a way to do that like Peter did?

WEEK 5 MARKAN PARABLES

The account of Mark, like that of the other evangelists, is characterized by parables. A parable is a common story, many times connected to the landscape or social situations the original audience was familiar with. The twist so to speak in a parable is that it contains a riddle, a dilemma, or an unexpected situation that shows God's answer to the plot, not what would be culturally expected. A parable is full of the possibility of an alternative and richer reality that God can offer us. Parables were found in the Old Testament, so they were an accepted method of teaching in Jesus' time. He used it masterfully to conceal messages about the kingdom of God, not to keep its availability to all limited, but to serve partly as a safety measure to the messianic secret until Jesus wanted his identity revealed. Of course, the fullness of that identity could only be understood after his passion and resurrection.

Seeds are effective metaphors for the kingdom. A metaphor is a literary device used to compare things that may not seem to be related to each other. They teach us something new about the reality of the compared items. After speaking in metaphors, Jesus retreated with his disciples to explain the parables privately to them for God's answer and possibilities are not easily understandable at first glance. Do we remember parables when we hear them over and over again yearly at Mass? Do we even grasp their meaning with repetition and explanation?

The first kingdom parable, and one unique to Mark's Gospel, of the seed growing silently and secretly, reveals the mystery of Jesus' mission to those who believed and embraced his mission. Framed within two other seed stories that are also found in other Gospels, this short parable is about the kingdom of God alive in the world now, like a seed. It is small, relatively unseen, and sprouts independent of human action. The sower scatters the seed randomly, but the rest is up to God. The emphasis in this parable is on the power of God that divinely guides the seed's growth to bring it to full harvest. While this is a kingdom parable, it is also a discipleship parable. Discipleship bears a bountiful harvest. God has his own time so there is no need for impatience. The kingdom will come. The meaning of the seed conceals the mystery of God. The other two seed parables talk about the type of soil the seed falls on, like the way the word of God takes root in people, and the size of the mustard seed, like the incipient word of God, that will grow like the mustard seed to become a very large tree.

Can we learn in Lent to be patient with the unfolding gift of the kingdom, seeing it slowly becoming, or do we have to tear into it in impatience? The seed needs warmth, light and love, and it receives it in God. The seed has an internal order that will allow it to become what it was meant to become under God's design. Contemplate a seed this Lent. It is designed to give forth life and fruit, and we are no less than the miracle of a seed.

WEEK 6 DISCIPLESHIP

Just after his Baptism in the Jordan and his emergence from the desert to enter his public life, Jesus took the initiative and chose his disciples with a sense of urgency. He needed them as helpers to share in his work. They responded to his unparalleled authoritativeness, and were single-minded in their response, for immediately they left everything to follow him.

Mark presented the twelve as somewhat obtuse. He purposely emphasized their faults and lack of understanding about who Jesus was, and the meaning of his ministry. While Mark depicts the disciples as dull, the demons that Jesus exorcised consistently knew his full identity, and the significance that his coming to bring in the kingdom meant the eventual end of their dominion. Repeatedly, the disciples needed to be told and retold things, and have those things interpreted and reinterpreted in order to understand. The unexpected elements that the disciples needed to learn from Jesus were not only that he was the Messiah, but also what *kind* of Messiah he was, and hence what it meant to be his follower. They were called to partake in his mission as witnesses who shared and assisted Jesus in the two essential elements of the call to discipleship—being with Jesus and doing the things of Jesus.

Discipleship, as evidenced through the Markan description of the disciples, seemed to be a failed attempt for they did not understand who was with them, his mission, or the suffering nature of true discipleship. But then again, Jesus was viewed as a failed Messiah too. As we saw, these initial failures to comprehend who Jesus was are captured in Mark through stories and images of blindness and then seeing through the restoration of sight and the gift of faith. He was amazed at their lack of faith yet despite their flaws, the point is they did follow him to the point of taking nothing for the journey except trust like their Old Testament ancestors. Following their commission, he gave them powers to preach, to anoint, and heal through exorcisms, and they did but Jesus always emphasized that the powers came through prayer to the father in faith.

In Mark, the realm of discipleship was larger than that of the twelve apostles, but included the blind, scribes, tax collectors, sinners, the healed demoniac, and the women who ministered to him and others. When Jesus tells them what will happen to him, they tried to talk him out of it. Does the cross really need to be taken up? But the kingdom quietly ushered in through Jesus was not achieved by military power or displayed by might, but through a discipleship of compassion, service, and suffering. Discipleship required a life of humility and humble service, inclusiveness, sacrifice, distance from the world, even death which was clarified when Jesus takes up the cross. Following Jesus to that end is the model of behavior—characteristics grounded in prayer and faith, essential to Jesus and to all Christians. Through his command over nature, demons, and people, Jesus is the "stronger one" in a precarious world of suffering that requires the refreshment and renewal of the spirit. In Lent let us rely and rest upon the shoulder of the stronger one who carried the cross of our salvation for us. What can we do in return as his disciples?

WEEK 7 THE HOLY SPIRIT

It was not Mark's purpose to elucidate upon the Holy Spirit, yet Mark clearly knew the spirit. In fact, organized theological treatises about the Trinity did not come into effect until the Middle Ages. However, Mark introduces the Holy Spirit matter of factly at the Baptism of Jesus, perhaps an index that the early post-Christian community was intimately acquainted with the spirit. Indeed, they lived in a spirit-filled period, well-familiar with the charisms that lead and infused the work of the church, versus an organized, hierarchal church structure. The Holy Spirit was the soul of the church, the spirit of love between the father and Jesus, and the instrument of the healing powers Jesus gave his disciples to use.

Like the first apostles, it is evident that the church has not always been able to understand who Jesus is. The kingdom of God had arrived, and is in the functional and symbolic space of the church, but defined by structures that are inherent to the nature of bureaucracy. Its character is cumbersome to work with and slow to change. Yet after two thousand years, the church is still sustained by the perseverance of the spirit, and the unseen scattered seed that sprouts under the power of God. While we might like some things to change immediately in the church such as increased empowerment for the laity in ministry, the ordination of women as deacons if not more, and the delivery of the sacrament of the anointing of the sick by lay persons as it was in early Christian times, we understand that the nature of growth is silent and slow. Studying and reflecting on Mark can temper our impatience as a disciple in the church. Mark's Gospel stories of the silent growing seed, and the blindness of Jesus' followers, help us to trust in the providence of God in the direction of the church though the Holy Spirit. The church is a servant to a reality greater to itself—God's kingdom, God's reign.

In hearing the terse eloquence of Mark we must realize that we are called to follow the one who suffered and died. Our discipleship is defined by his messiahship, that is, in terms obedience, suffering, and service. Jesus tells us in Mark, whatever you ask for in prayer and believe that you have it, it will be received. Can we believe in the power of the Holy Spirit to sustain us till the end of time? Prayer is the language of the Holy Spirit. Giving has a spirit and it is holy.

This Lent let us pray and learn about the Holy Spirit through the servanthood of Jesus. While the text says he retired to the desert, the historical–critical method reveals that there were no deserts in the proximity of Capernaum. More accurately the passage is interpreted as a lonely place. We all know lonely places, places of isolation and destruction. Yet we really aren't alone, it is impossible. Demons can claim us or angels minster to us. We can choose. Is there any choice? And if we choose, what does that mean but to go back out to world of servanthood, to experience suffering and even death. But this is the parabolic nature of things. Jesus showed us life comes from death. The Holy Spirit is with us until the end of time even in the lonely places that we must leave to experience the fullness of life that comes from the community of church and Christ. Come to the Easter Vigil, when the elect and we are movingly brought into that holy presence.

WEEK 8 EASTER IN MARK

Jesus has died, his suffering described in short and matter of fact terms. Mark is not content with the curtain of the stage being pulled closed at this final act. Paralleling the heavens opening at the Baptism of Jesus, as the skies darken, the veil of the temple is rent in two suggesting the end of the old covenant. And it is a Gentile, the Roman centurion, as he witnessed the death of Jesus on the cross, who recognized a truth that the chief priest could not accept. 'Truly this man was God's Son."

The women arrive in the early morning to continue to see the tomb but the stone is rolled away and the tomb is empty! These humble women who had come with Jesus from Jerusalem, and who had ministered to him in Galilee, and looked on from a distance as silent, faithful disciples in their ministry of presence at his death on the cross, are told by an angel that he has risen and has gone on ahead to Galilee as he said. The shortest Gospel comes to an end. Some say Mark didn't have a chance to finish the Gospel, so centuries later an alternate ending was added. But as an effective storyteller, Mark realized sometimes less is more. In Markan fashion, we have to fill in the rest, to answer the question as Bartimaeus, the disciples, the woman who anointed his head and feet with rich oil, the centurion and the early Christians did through their emotions of fear and awe. "Who do you say that I am?"

The hungry have been fed with the multiplication of loaves and fishes, the ill healed, the crowds taught by Jesus' word in perplexing yet pregnant parables of possibility, the passion predictions fulfilled. We have been told to be like children—we do not need status or power. We are important and loved. We know the end of the story yet we are still thrilled to hear it like a young child who pleads to hear the same tale over and over again, until he or she knows it by heart. Through its apocalyptic symbolism for the present age and the future, the early Christians were given so much to think about, act upon, and believe in that could change their world. Mark's is a story of the reality and role of suffering that even Jesus was not exempt from, an important theology to absorb.

Discipleship is journey with and to God that follows the messianic pattern. We learn that the way back to God is through suffering and love, just as it was the way for Jesus. We cannot distance ourselves from the cross for it is the way. In this manner, we can grow into the humanity and divinity of Jesus through an entire way of life. Along the way we may be blind. We cannot see everything from our limited perspective and experience. Through Jesus we are called to see the larger reality of existence, and for the most part, coming to see who Jesus is takes time. It is a gradual yet continual process of personal discernment formed by experience, conversation, service and prayer. Faith translates into sight, and that sight requires loving decision-making and action. Just as the seed gradually matures from blade to ear to full grain, the fullness of seeing takes time too. Faith is the light of God himself. It shows us the way to everlasting life through the clarity of John the Baptist crying in the desert and the centurion confessing that Jesus was the Son of God. Jesus is the seed, the secret, the "sight" and the suffering servant son of God. This is the joyous news of the Gospel of Jesus Christ proclaimed by the golden winged lion we call Mark. If we have understood this Lent the heart of Mark, we will surely arrive at the clear-sightedness of Easter morning! Blessed Easter to all!

8

The Fifty Days of Easter, Special Feast Days and Saints

Joyous decorations throughout the church

DIVINE MERCY SUNDAY: MANKIND WILL NOT HAVE PEACE UNTIL IT TURNS TO THE FOUNT OF MY MERCY*

Following the resurrection, the disciples hid in the locked upper room. Jesus appeared to them there and showed them the wounds from his side from which flowed blood and water when pierced at his crucifixion. At a later date, the apostle Thomas who was not with them, came to the room when Jesus appeared again, and placed his hands in those very wounds, and declared, "My Lord, and my God." This week is designated as Divine Mercy Sunday, a relatively new church feast, that has in common with the first Sunday after Easter the significance of those sacred wounds.

Maria Faustina Kowalska was born the third of ten children in Poland in 1905. With only three years of elementary school education, she left her family to work as a domestic servant, and at the age of twenty entered the Congregation of the Sisters of Our Lady of Mercy. She lived a simple life consisting of unassuming chores, but in the midst of cooking and gardening she united herself with Christ in a profoundly mystical way. In 1931 Jesus asked her to have his image painted as he appeared to her, with the adage, "Jesus, I trust in you," inscribed on it. In the picture we see the red and the pale rays emanating from his heart, symbolizing the blood of the cross and the waters of Baptism. In the apparition Jesus told her many profound things, but they all revolved around the incomprehensible and boundless mercy of his heart and the graces one would receive both from reverencing and imitating it. She died in 1938 at the age of thirty-three and was canonized on the first Sunday after Easter by Holy Father John Paul II in April 2000, the Sunday that would henceforth be called Divine Mercy Sunday.

This is an important day in the liturgical year, but due to its newness many people do not even know about it. On this day Jesus declared to Sr. Faustina in a private revelation accepted by the church the following. He said, on this day,

> All the divine floodgates through which graces flow are opened. The soul that goes to Confession and receives Holy Communion shall obtain the complete forgiveness of sins and punishment. When you go to confession, to this fountain of my mercy, the blood and water, which came forth from my heart, always flows down upon your soul. Every time you go to confession, immerse yourself entirely in my mercy with your great trust, so that I may pour the bounty of my grace upon your soul. When you approach

the confessional, know this, that I myself am waiting there for you. I am only hidden by the priest, but I myself act in your soul. Here the misery of the soul meets the God of mercy. Make your confession before me. The person of the priest is only a screen. Never analyze what sort of priest that I am making use of; open your soul in confession to me, and I will fill it with my light.

We are urged to be receptive to this plenary indulgence (complete forgiveness of sins and punishment**). In addition to the reception of those sacraments, veneration of the divine image and personal acts of mercy are encouraged. What a wonderful new feast and indulgence for the new millennium, an era fraught with so much suffering but so much sanctity if we contemplate and emulate his image. It returns our focus to the resurrection, and reminds us ultimately how to live with mercy. Let us join St. Thomas and St. Faustina in praise and adoration. "My Lord and My God." "Jesus, I trust in you."

*Revelation to St. Faustina found in her diary #699

**It is allowed to go to confession up to about 20 days before or after Divine Mercy Sunday

DIVINE MERCY SUNDAY: YOUR MERCY KNOWS NO BOUNDS (ALTERNATIVE VERSION)

As in the days of old, when God spoke to Abraham, Moses, and the prophets, and walked in the hills of Judea, he is still with us. He has not abandoned us; he is not an uninvolved distant God watching us dispassionately from afar, leaving us to our own foibles. God is the impetus of salvation history. He reaches out to us through his word, his son, the angels, saints, sacraments, and nature, and in everyone we meet. He longs for us as much or more than we long for him. We would not have this story without the lead character and it is he.

We learn about God slowly as consciousness emerges over time from our dusty origin. After the Fall we had to grapple with him in stages; we are too slow to catch on to all that he is. In the burning bush he revealed himself to Moses as a gracious God of mercy. In the beatitudes of the Gospel accounts he tells us, "Blessed are the merciful for they shall obtain mercy" (Matt 5:7). In post-New Testament days God revealed himself in apparitions to would-be saints personally and through his mother. He has always been merciful with a mercy so infinite we cannot even conceive of it. Slowly, at the right time, that mercy like his love comes shining through in history. So it was for the message of Divine Mercy.

In over six hundred pages of her diary, Maria Faustina Kowalska, an uneducated and unassuming young Polish nun, detailed her privileged graces of apparitions by Jesus that were eventually accepted by the church under the promptings of the Archbishop of Krakow, Karol Wojtya who later became Pope John Paul II. In his wisdom it was he who recognized the urgent and boundless love of Jesus for mankind and allowed her private revelations to be acknowledged. Years later he would canonize her on the day that is now known as Divine Mercy Sunday, the Sunday following Easter, on which we can further contemplate the immense love of God for his people. A plenary indulgence, which is the complete forgiveness of sins and punishment, can be gained by receiving the Sacrament of Reconciliation twenty days before or after Divine Mercy Sunday in combination with Holy Communion, venerating the divine image of his outpouring heart, and performing personal acts of mercy. This is an unfathomable invitation.

Instead of the burning bush or the transfiguration, Jesus comes to us with his blood and water pouring from his crucified heart. His mercy has certainly existed for all time, predating his apparitions to St. Faustina. In a world fraught with war and the threat of war, interpersonal problems and distress, the feast of Divine Mercy reveals, "Mankind will not have peace until it turns to the Fount of my Mercy." He is calling. Are we ready to hear the message?

THE FEASTS OF ST. ANSELM AND ST. MARK THE EVANGELIST: FOR A LITTLE TIME GIVE YOUR TIME TO GOD, AND REST IN HIM FOR A LITTLE (ANSELM'S *PROSLOGIUM*)

April 21 and April 25 respectively (may be during Lent)

Remembering back to the first week of Lent, we previewed Mark's account of the Gospel, and saw that his emphasis was on the passion of Christ. Now that Easter has arrived or just about, we commemorate the feast of St. Mark on April 25. Called "son" by Peter and companion to Paul, there is some question as to whether he was the young man in the garden when Jesus was arrested as well as several other New Testament characters, or if he, like Luke, did not know Jesus personally. He certainly knew the spirit of Jesus as conveyed by Peter whose teachings he documented. His image of John the Baptist as one howling in the desert became his insignia, that of the solitary golden winged lion.

Born in North Africa, Mark served as Bishop of Alexandria, Egypt, and is known as the Father of Christianity in Africa. After his martyrdom in Africa by those who feared he would replace their deities with the one true God, Mark's remains were surreptitiously smuggled to Venice under a slab of mutton that the Muslims would not touch. It is believed his body is entombed in the famed Basilica of San Marco in Venice, Italy while his head and no doubt his heart remained in Egypt.

Living apart by one thousand years, St. Anselm, whose feast is celebrated on April 21, was also a great writer. Born in northern Italy, he requested to enter the monastery as a young man, but was denied so as not to displease his father. After a carefree social life he became a monk, and quickly rose in the ecclesiastical ranks with wisdom not seen since the time of St. Augustine. He is one of the thirty-three Doctors of the Church and is accorded the title "Father of Scholasticism" since the scope of his writings covered the whole dogmatic field of Catholicism. He is best known for his work on why God became man, the most complete exposition on the Incarnation. He became the Archbishop of Canterbury, England, and fought many political battles with the wayward English kings.

From Egypt to Italy and from Italy to England, these prolific scribes were blessed with the graces of the spirit to craft the written word. Mark's golden lion proudly crowns the basilica that overlooks the teeming waterways of Venice, and equally welcomes the humble pigeons and throngs of tourists who crowd his plaza. Dante placed Anselm in the highest echelon of light and wisdom in his *Paradisio*. Saints Mark and Anselm are unquestionably at Jesus' side for the way they made the world know the son of God made man through their golden words.

WORLD DAY OF PRAYER FOR VOCATIONS AND THE FEAST OF ST. JOSEPH THE WORKER: BUT THE PLAN OF THE LORD STANDS FOREVER (PS 33:11)

FOURTH SUNDAY OF EASTER AND MAY 1 RESPECTIVELY

On the fourth Sunday of Easter we celebrate World Day of Prayer for Vocations. May 1 is the Feast of St. Joseph as the worker. St. Joseph's feast day commemorating his birthday and role as husband to Mary was celebrated on March 19. May Day, May 1, he is honored as the Catholic alternative to the original Communist holiday of May 1, now known as International Worker's Day. Today May 1 is associated globally with all work and more recently with immigration in the United States.

We think of St. Joseph, husband to the Blessed Virgin Mary and the earthly father of Jesus, as the just, righteous man who cared for and protected them. Of royal lineage of the house of David, his profession of carpenter did not reflect his noble descent as accurately as his regal humility did. He fashioned wood with his skilled hands and eye, no doubt as carefully as he tended his holy family, never anticipating that the wood he worked on to earn an earthly income would be the substance of the cross that his son would die on to earn eternal life for all.

Work has always had value. It is a way in which we serve others, for humanity is community with others. Even those who are in monasteries or cloisters serve us and each other by their prayers and acts of sacrifice. Work is not punishment but a way we express our unique God-given spirit and gifts. In many cultures work is assigned or is a function of one's status, but in God's eye, if it is work that is just, it is the way we further help in the completion of creation and the realization of the kingdom. In these difficult economic times work perhaps becomes more valued than ever, not just as a fundamental reality as a means of paying bills and making ends meet, but also for the sense of self-worth that it conveys. The loss of sense of purpose can be threatened by unemployment and destroys many people if their spirit is not anchored in God's will for them.

One of The World Day of Prayer for Vocations themes by Pope Benedict XVI, is expressed in *Faith in the Divine Initiative—the Human Response.* The emphasis of this day has always been on the importance of prayer for vocations to the priesthood and the consecrated life, and our religious are indispensable for the continuation of the church and the administration of the sacraments. But all vocations are equal in the sense of the universal call to holiness. We need our religious as our spiritual leaders, to help us become holy, and Pope Benedict, in the spirit of St. Paul, urges us to humbly respond to the call begun by God.

We have no recorded words of St. Joseph in scripture or any other works, and yet he has certainly taught us a lot about how to be a virtuous and caring person through our work. While our labors are necessary, important and do matter, in the end it is not so much what we do as how we do it that will make a difference to the world when it is done for the glory of God.

THE FEAST OF OUR LADY OF FATIMA: MY IMMACULATE HEART WILL NEVER ABANDON YOU (FATIMA REVELATION)

MAY 13

We all know the story of almost one hundred years ago when our Blessed Virgin Mary appeared to the three poor children in Fatima, Portugal as they were tending sheep. We may or may not precisely remember the Fatima messages which were astounding at the time—the conversion of Russia from Communism, the last revealed secret of the attempted assassination of a would-be pope who turned out to be John Paul II, and the importance of penance, prayer, and devotion to the Immaculate Heart of Mary in the form of the rosary for the salvation of all.

Fatima is second to Lourdes as the most visited shrine in the world and its story is immortalized in the minds of those who have made personal visits there as well as through humble, touching movies. We see in this apparition that is more than a personal revelation that Mary, Jesus, and the angels continue to visit the poor, the lowly, and the uneducated and are entrusted with world-changing messages. But since its prophecies have come to pass, what is the continued allure of, and the relevant, enduring message of Fatima?

For all times Fatima's poignant promise points to the power of the rosary that incorporates the mysteries of our salvation. They honor Mary as the mother of the Incarnate God who not only was born historically but also is present in the Eucharist at Mass and reserved for adoration. It is not coincidental that the Feast of Our Lady of the Blessed Sacrament was celebrated on this same day before Mary made her repeated visits to the children. As the Mother of God she invites us to meet her son through her.

One understated way that Mary points out the evil of sin is the incident of two young girls who had died that the children knew and asked about. Mary responded that one was in heaven but the other child would be in purgatory to the end of time unless others saved her through the intercession of prayer. What sins could be so great that this would be the fate of a child or is it that this is the true measure of sin? If a child's sins are so great, what about our own as adults who have lived so many more years and sinned so much more? This is a heavy statement about the weight and consequence of sin that we should ponder.

On this feast of Our Lady of Fatima, let us understand and appreciate the natural love of a mother for us as children, and the love of our Blessed Mother, so much so that she could change the cosmos with the miracle of the sun to prove her divine emissary role. In the wake of Divine Mercy Sunday, let us be grateful for only the mercy that can save us, and live the message of Fatima for ourselves and for the child in purgatory that is in all of us.

SPECIAL TOPIC—ST. DAMIEN JOSEPH DE VEUSTER OF MOLOKA'I: BELGIAN, HAWAIIAN AND AMERICAN SAINT— I AM A LEPER, BLESSED BE THE GOOD GOD (DAMIEN)

May 10

Joseph de Veuster, the youngest of seven children, was born in Belgium to a farming family in 1840. He desired to become a priest with the Congregation of the Sacred Hearts of Jesus and Mary, a missionary sect in Hawaii. Two months after his arrival in Honolulu, he was ordained there in Our Lady of Peace Cathedral. After years of service on the Big Island of Hawaii, he joined the exiled lepers on the island of Moloka'i on May 10, 1873 and this date is his universal memorial date. In the most remote islands of the world, beneath its steepest sea cliffs, on the isolated peninsula of Kalaupapa, Father Damien devoted his life to the lepers who were ostracized from their homes, their culture, and every social institution in this segregated colony. Like the lepers of most history including New Testament times, their contagion was feared, and the stigma of being a leper incurred social and spiritual rejection, and stripping the ill patients of the basic dignities of a human being that Damien restored. It was to this end that Damien humbly and heroically gave his strong body and his entire heart.

Lepers arrived to the barren island, if they survived being thrown into the wild, dangerous waters, from the ships they were transported in. Many perished in this cruel and torturous way, but to those who were rescued Fr. Damien quietly ministered to the abandoned, quarantined islanders day and night. Here there was no housing, no food, no medicine, simply nothing but disfigured, rejected people, and the boundless love of a foreign priest, his presence as constant as the tropical sun, his touch as gentle, calm, and loving as the ocean breeze. Here Damien created social order in a place of lawlessness, buried the dead left to the dogs, converted shacks to cottages, cultivated crops, secured basic medicines, promoted education, art and music, constructed a church, a school, an orphanage and a hospital, built roads and a dock, instituted Catholic liturgy, and administered the sacraments. He was the motive force and social glue of every aspect of their intimate daily life, and the source of hope to all over time as he replaced their despair with unconditional love.

He unrelentingly bathed their contorted bodies and bound their wounds knowing he too would succumb someday to the disease as he did sixteen years later. Like St. Paul, he boasted of his love of God when he wrote, "I make myself a leper with the lepers to gain all to Jesus Christ." Even though the church and the Hawaiian government before it was part of the United States sent him to care for these outcasts, there were those who despised his work and thwarted his attempts to care for his beloved abandoned flock, and he experienced great personal isolation after he was rejected as a leper himself. Eventually his work became further known, and Hawaiian royalty and foreign doctors visited the island to witness his goodness. For those who thought life was over it had really just begun through his loving hand that touched them on every level.

He produced a beautiful choir that joyfully and heartbreakingly sang even though their vocal cords barely existed due to the devastation of the disease, and he promoted indigenous sports to the fun loving Hawaiians even when they had no feet, which the disease had claimed. One of his greatest accomplishments was to bring the small group of Franciscan nuns, whom he always wanted to join him, to sustain the budding culture to Moloka'i. Under the supervision of Blessed Marianne of Syracuse, New York they came to risk their own lives and live out the love of God. To this day not one sister has suffered from this disease as he promised and Marianne is on her way to canonization.

Fr. Damien died at the age of 49 of the tropical bacterial disease of leprosy that is now called Hansen's disease. He was beatified in 1995 and on October 11, 2009 canonized in Rome. Eight Kalaupapa patients from Moloka'i traveled to Belgium and then to Rome in great joy to honor as a saint the man who tenderly held their dying ancestors all night beneath the bended palm trees in wind, cold, heat and rain, and welcomed their suffering as his own. Somewhere between heaven and earth, in the middle of a vast ocean, Damien witnessed he understood the Hawaiian spirit of *Aloha* that is God.

THE FEAST OF THE ASCENSION: I WILL SEE YOU AGAIN AND YOUR HEARTS WILL REJOICE AND NO ONE WILL TAKE YOUR JOY AWAY FROM YOU (JOHN 16:22)

It is Ascension Thursday, a day unlike any other because it commemorates the ascension of our Lord into heaven. Can you imagine witnessing the resurrection and then see Jesus rise to heaven! At this point things never seen before continue to surprise the apostles. Their joy must be so great. This man continues to prove he is God. On that day it always seems the clouds are bigger, piled high like a staircase to heaven, the sunlight is more beautiful. There is a miraculous golden pink horizon, a true ascension skyline.

The Ascension is described in Mark and Luke's Gospels, and the Acts of the Apostles by St. Luke. It is the second Glorious Mystery of the rosary and a tenet of our faith that we express at Mass in the Creed. The hill where the Ascension is believed to have taken place is Mount Olivet near Jerusalem. St. Helena, who found the true cross, had a memorial constructed here, and there were basilicas built as well that were repeatedly destroyed. On this day the Paschal candle is extinguished from our presence but will be used throughout the year for baptisms and funerals, and lighting the Advent wreath, signifying our life in Christ. Christ has ascended to the father, his mission completed. It is a day of great rejoicing, for while the visible Christ of history is no longer with us, things are irrevocably changed. He remains behind with us in the form of his precious body and blood given to us at Mass and reserved for adoration, and in his church through the Holy Spirit, the soul of the church. The kingdom of heaven is at hand. The period of waiting is over.

While customs have changed over time, current liturgical protocols instruct us on how to receive the post-resurrection Christ. When we come forward for Communion, whether we receive the host, the precious blood or both, it is important to remember that each species is complete. It is his body and blood, soul and divinity that we accept under the roof of our mouth, or in our extended, cuplike hands, or from the cup. It is appropriate to allow the Minister of Holy Communion to place the host in our hands and not to take it from them. It is not Roman Catholic custom to intincture the host, meaning we do not dip it in the precious blood. We say, "*Amen*," (I believe), not any other word, upon acknowledgement to the phrase by the minister, "the Body of Christ" or "the Blood of Christ," and make a slight bow. We receive communion standing as a sign of honor to God and thereby create a unified assembly of the Body of Christ that is the church that he is head of. There is no need to genuflect or look around the minister searching for the altar, the empty tabernacle, or the immobile cross. Christ, God, is right in front of us, cradled in our hands or received into our mouth. Yes, it is a mystery we cannot understand.

The Ascension is one of our Holy Days of Obligation, somewhat underplayed since it is transferred in many locations to the subsequent Sunday, but its celebration and meaning is no less important. He came gloriously and quietly to Mary in her womb, and now leaves the only way he can, in her presence and that of the apostles as he ascends to the father. He will come again in glory to judge the living and the dead and of his kingdom there will be no end.

PENTECOST: RECEIVE THE HOLY SPIRIT (JOHN 20:22)

In many places it sometimes seems that there are five seasons: wind, fire, cold, dryness and rain. So perhaps we shouldn't be surprised when wind and fire collide like clouds cavorting in the skies at the transition of the seasons and the time of Pentecost. Buddhist prayer flags bend to their knees; tumbleweeds like prisoners released from jail run and reclaim their lives. Tongues of fire that light or scathe the world are our choice. The elements of wind and fire engender and sustain each other.

Wind is a master of disguise and a major biblical theme to express the work of God, invisible but no less real. Winds can be tropical and balmy, gentle and quiet, hot, cold or dry, as forceful as a hurricane, a northeaster or a tornado, or annoying as a mosquito, but they make their presence known and affect us. Winds of war, winds of change, mighty winds, whirlwinds, scorching winds, stormy winds, they are not neutral. They scatter seeds, allergens, pathogens and moisture, refresh and heal, and devastate or destroy. The breath of spring wind signifying the power of God stirs us that great things can happen. God speaks to his creatures through his creation.

It is Pentecost Sunday, fifty days after the resurrection, and for Christians, the birth of the church. In Old Testament times Pentecost was the day of the Jewish festival of the Feast of Weeks, celebrating the first fruits of the harvest fifty days after the Passover. Later, liturgically it commemorated the fifty days after the departure from Egypt when Moses was given the Law on Mount Sinai. In France on this day, the wind of trumpets are played, and in Italy, rose petals, a wind of soft fragrant beauty and fiery color, are dropped from the ceilings of the churches signifying the tongues of fire that descended upon the apostles. Red for love and those tongues of fire is the color of Pentecost. Floral flames of scarlet gladiolas ascend from the baptismal font, the waters of life, and the adornment of redheaded ginger and birds of paradise point to the cross and the altar of salvation.

Imagine that first Pentecost! The disciples have witnessed Jesus in his public life, followed him sorrowfully to Calvary, met him in the upper room, and have seen his wounds and watched him gloriously ascend into heaven. Is there any doubt who this man is? And now his spirit descends upon them in a wind with tongues of fire. They are no longer the same, emboldened to take to the streets, travel the world under perilous conditions to reach the ends of the earth known at that time, write gospels and epistles, and die as martyrs for Jesus Christ, the Messiah, the son of God, who has come. They are commissioned to make disciples of all nations. Nothing could be more important for this is the Good News.

What will it take for us to follow him so unequivocally? Can we allow the Holy Spirit to take over us in a holy wind and a sacred flame lighting our minds and hearts? Will we let him stir us up until the end of time? What type of wind have you been? What type of wind do you want to be—a wind that sighs and moans or sings; one that dances or destroys, whispers or wails, gets caught in a sail; one that reaches beyond forgiveness to reconciliation? Think back to the anticipation of your confirmation when as a young adult you chose Christ and he sent his spirit upon you. Think of your confirmation name and its significance for you then and now. Is it a powerful wind for you? Invite the Holy Spirit to dwell in your soul through the tongues of fire and the winds of possibility, that through their commingling, ignite a life-giving love. With the spirit we participate in salvation history. Come Holy Spirit fill the hearts of Thy faithful.

9

Ordinary Time Resumes

The baptismal font in Ordinary Time

THE FEAST OF THE MOST HOLY TRINITY: GLORY BE TO THE FATHER AND TO THE SON AND TO THE HOLY SPIRIT

O RDINARY TIME HAS RESUMED. The last time it was celebrated was the first Sunday before Ash Wednesday. It seems like a long time ago. Since the beginning of the liturgical year we have been advented, lented, and repented. We have traveled the twenty decades of the rosary, the mysteries of our faith. It is now the end of the feasting of the Easter season, the way things will henceforth be until the church year ends in late November or early December. It is a sweet slice of heaven.

It is no liturgical coincidence that the Feast of the Holy Trinity follows on the heels of Pentecost. With the Holy Spirit still fresh in our minds from the riot of red at Pentecost, and the Ordinations, Confirmations, First Eucharists and Baptisms of May, he is now celebrated, not singularly, but in the Mystery of the Holy Trinity, the core of all Catholic doctrine, a mystery of unity that should connect us with its love, not divide or destroy churches, families, or nations through heresy or disbelief.

In the movie *Million Dollar Baby,* a weathered and introspective Clint Eastwood, aged yet enriched since the slick *Dirty Harry* days, emerging from daily Mass, accosts the presiding priest and tells the priest he's not sure that he understand the Trinity. His priest matter of factly responds, apparently used to his parishioner's devote yet grabbling faith, that it is not something to be understood and he is right. The dogma of the Trinity is the root of our faith. Without revelation we would not have discovered it, yet even in that promulgation it retains the inscrutability of mystery. So too it is the appropriate attitude towards the Holy Trinity: one to accept and hold in awesome incomprehension letting its richness envelope us and deepen with every passing day and year. As divine revelation it is not in our power to explain, or reason, yet there is something inherent in Catholicism that allows us to accept it as naturally as the rising and setting of the sun along with all of the other mysteries that make up our faith—the Immaculate Conception of Mary, the Incarnation of Jesus, his crucifixion, death, and resurrection. That must be the faith part of it, a mysterious truth that once revealed seems to make sense for a God with all the qualities we would expect God to have—a triune, united, indivisible yet distinct God of love.

The anthropomorphic, paternal God the father, and the divinely human Jesus may be easier to relate to as persons and we may have a closer relationship with them because of their existence in the Bible and in human history. The Holy Spirit may descend like a dove at Baptism, or under the tongues of fire at Pentecost, symbolic of a new reality, and yet the Holy Spirit is inseparable from the father and the son. We know he is with us in liturgy and daily life and especially when we love, for love, like ours, is their origin, common denominator, and eternal destiny.

THE SOLEMNITY OF THE MOST HOLY BODY AND BLOOD OF CHRIST (CORPUS CHRISTI): THIS IS MY BODY WHICH IS BEING GIVEN UP FOR YOU (LUKE 22:19)

It seems appropriate that the Feast of Corpus Christi follows the Feast of the Holy Trinity, giving special honor to God the son, just as the Feast of Pentecost gave honor to God the Holy Spirit. Corpus Christi, a resplendent feast, initiated in honor of the institution of the sacrament of the Eucharist on Holy Thursday, is celebrated variously around the world. While processions might be more expected in small European villages as quaint vestiges of the past, in today's era in the United States and in many parishes, a procession in which the body of Christ is brought from the holy tabernacle of the church into the streets is a bold act of public faith. The monstrance, holding the body of Christ under the species of the pale host, is carried to the places of our everyday commerce, where he belongs in every social act that we do. It is an act that Christ himself instructed in his revelations to St. Juliana in the twelfth century that he would like continually honored when he said, "I desire another day to be set apart in which it shall be celebrated by the whole of Christendom," referring to a day for adoring and appreciating the Eucharist.

Many saints over time have had an especial devotion to the adoration of the Blessed Sacrament including St. Alphonsus Liguori, St. Thomas Aquinas, St. Francis of Assisi, and so many others. They appreciated the enormous gift of his continued presence with us in the church following his ascension, an unprecedented, continued company even the unique period of the prophets and God's chosen people of Old Testament times were not privy to. He has left his body, his Holy Spirit, and his church for us until he comes again.

The mystery of the indivisible body and blood of Christ, under the appearance of the basic foodstuffs of bread and wine, is not symbolic, but truly transubstantiated from now until the end of time, brought down to us daily, hourly, in every celebration of the Mass around the world, to feed us on our journey to heaven. It is a food that brings Jesus into our body on the spiritual and cellular level. We can receive Christ's body at Mass, or adore during First Friday or Perpetual Adoration, or journey with him figuratively or literally on the Feast of his Most Precious Body and Blood.

The whole world needs to be fed by the body of Christ. How will this happen with the paralyzing paucity of priests? Celibacy is a holy, special state of life that allows for a concentrated devotion to God that we need from our priests as a people journeying to him. Will more men come forward to devote their lives singularly to God as a priest or as a single or married deacon? Finding one's vocation to the priesthood or deaconate may not be easy unless we as a church socially and culturally value that state of life. We pray for vocations, but maybe our limitations and our results are a function of our prayer, as the scriptures say we are not praying as we ought. Or maybe we are not hearing the answers to that prayer through an adherence to an outmoded patriarchal paradigm. St. Benedict beautifully defined work as what we do penetrated by prayer. As laity we are the limbs of the Body of Christ, he is our head, our priests are its organs and Mary its heart. What will you, what can we do to keep that body alive? Let us pray!

THE FEAST OF THE SACRED HEART OF JESUS AND THE FEAST OF THE IMMACULATE HEART OF MARY: THEN HE SAID TO HIS DISCIPLE, "BEHOLD, YOUR MOTHER" (JOHN 19:26)

As we know, Mary has countless titles that reflect her numerous roles in the life of the church. We may relate to some more than others based upon where we live in the world, or under the title by which she has most affected us. But her central role as Jesus' mother is surely tantamount to any as it is the primal relationship of a mother to her child, expressing a heart that by nature is only love. Her pure heart is not something that we have to believe in, it is so easy to accept, for how could she be anything else?

Like Jesus' sacred heart we have somewhat analogous devotions to Mary's heart, which is sacred too, but more commonly referred to as immaculate reflecting the purity derived from her immaculate conception in which she was conceived devoid of sin. That quality of her heart continued to be cultivated as Jesus' mother, brimming with the silent humble joy of being the Mother of God, and further made radiant through the sorrows and tears that accompanied watching him fulfill his mission as God's only son. Hence her heart is depicted with flames and a circle of thorns.

There are many parishes, religious orders, songs, prayers, and devotions celebrating her purity. Lucia Santos, the oldest of the children of Fatima, became a sister of the Immaculate Heart of Mary upon Mary's direction. In fact, if we remember, Mary at Fatima divulged to the children that the last two remedies to save the world that was so offending God with its sins, and to save souls, was to pray the rosary daily and to be devoted to her Immaculate Heart. From this revelation came the devotions to Mary in the form of the First Saturdays. In this tradition, on the First Saturday of the month, Mary requested that we do four things:

1. Confess sins
2. Receive Holy Communion
3. Recite and meditate on five decades of the rosary and
4. Spend fifteen minutes with her praying for the reparation of sin.

In exchange for this she promises to be with us at the hour of our death, at our side, with the grace-filled vault of her heart. First Saturday is a wonderful practice that we can integrate into our lives and combine with the First Friday devotions the day before if we structure our time and make these commitments. But no external devotion to Mary or Jesus in the form of rosaries, medals or scapulars is meaningful if it does not lead to an interior conversion of behavior.

Back to back, these two feasts celebrate the same thing—the hearts of Mary and Jesus inextricably connected to each other. Their dual hearts of the same flesh, unfathomable, unconditional, immaculate and sacred, eternally entwined on vines of love, extend to us. Mary, the mother and heart of the church, given to us through St. John at the foot of the cross at the death of her son, grants us life that can only come from the heart.

THE NATIVITY OF ST. JOHN THE BAPTIST:
ECCE AGNUS DEI—BEHOLD, THE LAMB OF GOD!
(JOHN 1:29)

JUNE 24

One the happiest incidents in New Testament writings is the moment when St. John the Baptist leaps in his mother Elizabeth's womb upon meeting Mary carrying the baby Jesus in her own womb. John, six months younger than Jesus his cousin, as a growing child in his mother's body, knows God when he is in his presence. It is an image of overflowing joy, one that should make our hearts leap too at the thought of it. Does that ever happen to us when we see God in others? Have we forgotten how to leap for joy?

Three nativities are commemorated in the liturgical year, and John's nativity is the oldest feast day of the church. In addition to the births of Jesus and Mary, John's nativity is an illustration of his importance in the life of the church and the hierarchy of the saints. Usually the dates of the deaths of saints are celebrated, commemorating their entrance to heaven, but the aforementioned nativities concern the entry of the Holy Spirit into the lives of his blessed mother and an unparalleled prophet. In six months it will be the nativity of Jesus again!

Religious art is rich in depictions of St. John the Baptist especially in his ministry by the Jordan and his beheading. Lesser-known precious paintings of Mary holding him, and of John playing in the company Mary, Elizabeth, and his childhood companion, Jesus, makes one so happy to behold. He is frequently shown alongside a lamb denoting Jesus as the future sacrificial lamb.

Born to Zachary and Elizabeth in old age it is said that John left home when very young and retired to the desert to atone for sins and to prepare for his role of preaching. He then began baptizing those awaiting the Messiah. A strong, confident, and charismatic man, a Pentecostal personage forged of camel's hair, locusts, and wild honey, he was filled with the spirit. He got down to basics in dress and demeanor, his personal austerity matching his prophetic words. He was a whirlwind personality, gathering many and diverse peoples to him with his holy message. His public life cleared the way for the public life of Jesus to begin when Jesus too presented himself for Baptism. John made straight the path to the

Lord, making it easy for people to come to Jesus. Are there people in our lives who do this for us? Can we be one of them?

John is present in the First Luminous Mystery of the rosary via Jesus' Baptism in the Jordan, the Second Joyful Mystery, the Visitation. He is highlighted at Advent as the harbinger of the coming of the Messiah, and in the Mass at the Communion Rite when the priest says, *"Behold the Lamb of God who takes away the sins of the world. Happy are those who come to His supper."* In Mass it is one of those profound, happy moments when our hearts should leap to in love at the presence of our Savior.

THE FEAST OF ST. THOMAS THE APOSTLE: MY LORD AND MY GOD! (JOHN 20:28)

JULY 3

Just like the moment when St. John the Baptist leapt in his mother's womb at the recognition of Jesus, sometimes we too have brief moments when another person really knows us for who we are. Even though most of us live in a vastly interconnected world, we don't always see each other as a whole person or in their essence, as that interconnection actually leads to a fragmentation of our naked nature. But when we do have that clarity, it has great significance for us. It is as if we see in the other's recognition of us a mirror of our nature, and in that moment we are made humble and happy for our unique gifts from God. In that realization we grasp its significance and there is no turning back.

So it was for St. Thomas, one of the twelve apostles, who we remember for his incredulity that Christ had risen. But Thomas was one of those who asked what might have seemed like the "silly" questions we sometimes ask, and yet there are no stupid questions if we need them to be answered, for in their posing, we are searching for the truth. Thomas had the humility and the courage to ask such questions.

Some of the most important truths about Jesus were evoked from Thomas' candid questioning. Thomas asked, "Lord we do not know where we are going, how can we know the way?" (John 14:5). Do we remember the answer? Jesus responded, "I am the way, the truth, and the life" (John 14:6). Maybe some people just know that answer because God is so present in their lives, but most of us from childhood, through our teens and into adult life ask ourselves that question more than once as we stumble and fall through the journey of life. Eventually it sinks in with the bearable lightness of faith and then to do anything other than the obvious, is to go against the grain of our very being for we were made in God's image.

Thomas was away a lot, apparently doing work for the apostles, and so he tended to be late. While the other disciples were present in the upper room to see the risen Jesus he was not, and when Mary was assumed into heaven art depicts Thomas running through the hills on his way to join the others but he misses that too. This time though he doesn't doubt what has occurred, but just in case, Mary in her beneficence appears to him privately and gives him the belt of her garment, like a wise mother who knows the nature of her child and accepts him without reproach. The great painter Caravaggio shows Thomas putting his fingers not only on Jesus' superficial wounds but also directly into his flesh, a scene somewhat reminiscent of Adam reaching out to touch God the father to receive life in the creation scene of Michelangelo's famed ceiling of the Cistine Chapel.

"Blessed are those who have not seen and yet believe," (John 20:29) Jesus responded in connection to Thomas's doubt, but Thomas showed us the way to Jesus through his doubt. Jesus is the answer to his questions and ours. That answer is summed up in Thomas' succinct, familiar, famous, and eternal words of praise, "My Lord and My God!" (John 20:28) St. Thomas was martyred in India, his doubt undoubtedly the steppingstone to his faith.

THE FEAST OF ST. BENEDICT OF NURSIA: *ECCE! LABORA!* GO AND WORK! (BENEDICT)

JULY 11

In a period of turmoil and difficulty such as there is now in the world with the constant threat of war, unrest, daily violence, economic challenges, and changing social mores there is sometimes the wish to run away from it all. So much of history has been this way. In the fifth century AD, Benedict of Nursia, Italy, born into a family of means, even felt the same way. Giving up the glamour of Rome, he sought solace first in a smaller town and then later in a more extreme manner by living as a hermit in a cave where local monks had to bring him food. There Benedict realized the importance of merging both Gospel values, especially the maxims of the Sermon on the Mount, with the human need to be a person knitted in community, thus fulfilling our social, people-of-God nature.

Leaving the cave, Benedict as a layperson, became a leader and founded twelve monasteries, which were more like households, as this was Benedict's concept of how one should live. His awareness of the importance of balance in one's life led to his formation of what has become known as *The Rule*, essentially a prescription for a healthy life. Originally the rule was designed for the layperson living in community, and later took on its clerical association. The essence of the rule consisted of a life of charity, fraternity, work, prayer, and worship, all in the context of moderation. There were no vows of poverty. Benedict said everyone should have what they need: ample sleep, abundant food and wine, sufficient and varied clothing. Moderation sounds like a luxury and for most of the world it would be today.

Benedict elevated or perhaps perceived the correct nature of work in the world. It was not a punishment as a consequence of original sin, but the universal lot of man, a means of goodness, necessary for his well-being, and essential for him as a Christian. In fact, Benedict went so far as to say that work comes before prayer but that prayer should infuse and penetrate work. Liturgy and public prayer should be pure, short, even wordless he said, and private prayer he left to the individual. He conceived of prayer as the source and center of life, an invitation to find the world in God. Fifteen hundred years later the rule sounds like a practical way for us to live our busy, fractured lives. It is the spirit and sustenance of our temperate work and existence.

Benedict was blessed with the power of prophecy, the ability to perform miracles, and he had the unique privilege of having a vision of God. His sister and perhaps twin St. Scholastica lived in a comparable community, and when she died he happily saw her soul arise to heaven as a dove from his monastery at Monte Cassino. Benedict is one of the six patron saints of Europe but his influence persists to this day beyond that continent in what we could call his application of practical religion. St. Benedict is depicted carrying a simple bundle of twigs, symbolic of the rule, perhaps a reminder that God, invisible and present, can be found in the sacred mundane world where we live for it is his creation.

BLESSED KATERIE TEKAKWITHA AND THE FEAST OF ST. BONAVENTURE: O GOOD FORTUNE!

J̲U̲L̲Y̲ ̲1̲4̲ ̲A̲N̲D̲ ̲J̲U̲L̲Y̲ ̲1̲5̲ ̲R̲E̲S̲P̲E̲C̲T̲I̲V̲E̲L̲Y̲

Each saint has something special to teach us, each saint lives in some special way, holding God in his or her being. Whether it is the "little way" of St. Therese of Lisieux, St. Benedict's philosophy of work and prayer, St. Paul's passionate evangelism, or St. John the Baptist's preaching in the desert, they each mirror and honor God through the unique capacity and configuration of their one-of-a-kind soul. It is likewise true that the compelling truth of the Incarnation surpasses cultures and continents as our nature seeks truth and to know our creator. So it is with the celebration of two gentle saints this month, the Blessed Katerie Tekakwitha of North America, and St. Bonaventure of Tuscany, Italy, born over four hundred years apart and over four thousand miles away from each other.

Saints speak to us in common and in different ways depending upon what we know about them as a whole or how our individual interests perceive them. Katerie was a simple, young girl, a virginal convert to Christianity in a time when the white man's God was not presented in the fullness of his mercy but under the guise of zealous warring nations. When she did convert to the holy Catholic Church she devoted herself to prayer and fasting for the good of her nation. She took the commandments seriously by abstaining from work on Sunday to the point that her people would not feed her because she did not labor. She was a girl not just marked by smallpox but with the purity of faith lived out quietly and humbly in her short life, and her even shorter time as a baptized child of God.

In a fast-paced, modern culture we might think this commandment has gone out of fashion, that Sunday is a day just like any other, even a day that one does not need to go to Mass because our individual relationship to God surpasses the requirements of organized religion, never mind a day when one does not work. But the commandment to keep holy the Lord's day, came from God, and its observance has great grace-filled significance for us personally, for our families, friends, parish, community, and the world if we observe it the way God intended. We might even enjoy the respite of rest, the fraternity of family and friends visiting each other, the special Sunday foods, the change of pace, and the mental and physical nourishment that can come from celebrating Sunday. Would we, like Katerie, give up our meals in lieu of the cultural expectation to do what the world expects?

Then there is Bonaventure, great prolific Doctor of the Church, contemporary of St. Thomas Aquinas, and Franciscan friar with a biography so long and accomplishments for the church so great that we can only be awed by his understanding of theology and his holy example. A scholar who left behind *The Life of St. Francis*, five hundred sermons, the epitome of Scholastic writings, yet the reputation of being a warm, "angelic," scholar who performed miracles but thought they were less important than the imitation of the Lord. Bonaventure, a man who like Katerie, was generous, kind, compassionate and fervent, on a brief, unknown, tumultuous journey to God that is our journey as well. His name says it all—*O good fortune!*

THE FEAST OF ST. JAMES THE GREATER, APOSTLE: SON OF THUNDER

July 25

St. James the Greater, an apostle—he was a powerful man, full of authority and even some self-importance—a lot like us. Hence Jesus called him and his brother, who were sons of Zebedee, "sons of thunder." His fiery ego wouldn't want to be confused with James the Lesser, also an apostle who wrote the Letter of St. James of the New Testament. He was the brother of St. John the evangelist, the author of one of the Gospels, and a fisherman. Along with John and Peter he was favored with the incredible privilege of witnessing the Transfiguration, the Agony in the Garden, and the rising of Jarius' daughter recounted in the Gospel.

Legend has it that St. James left Jerusalem to go to Spain, bringing the Gospel west of his homeland to evangelize the Moors. Wearing his cap and cloak, he carried his staff, his gourd for water, and the Gospel book in which he is described. Later returning to his birthplace James lost his life as the first martyr for our faith, beheaded in Jerusalem by a sword, to appease the Jews.

James is immortalized in the Gospel, and in paintings he rides silver stallions in Spain or walks confidently with the breeze filling his long, youthful hair. He is depicted with scallop shells symbolizing his successful trek to the seacoast of Spain. A pilgrimage that continues to this day from medieval times is the journey of pilgrims to Santiago de Compostella to honor the presumed relic of his body in a tomb, however there is some legend affixed to both his journey to Spain as well as the authenticity of his remains. Legend or not what is significant is the journey of faith.

Even though we may travel and go on pilgrimages most of us will not be like James or any of the apostles who left their homes to spread the Gospel. Yet even our circumscribed lives are a journey that takes us from getting up every morning, through the toil of the day, to the evening when we are forced to stop and sleep, but our mandate is the same. What will we take with us on the journey that will aid us in getting to that land we believe in? Is our cell phone, our car, our lipstick, our water bottle or our coffee-to-go cup our scallop shell? Do we like James have an insignia that sums up our lives?

Most of us will not be martyrs in the traditional sense like the beheaded James. Sometimes all we can control is our head and even that can be taken away. What will we have to forfeit—the hair on our head from chemotherapy, our smooth skin to melanoma, friendships broken by our failings and misunderstandings, persecutions and injustices at the hands of envious enemies, broken hearts by spouses who no longer care?

If a water bottle can last one thousand years in a landfill, how much longer will our souls last! Can we pick up a shell from a holiday vacation and hear the faint but no less real calling of God? This summer is a good time to try. Can you hear the thunder?

THE FEASTS OF ST. IGNATIUS LOYOLA AND ST. ALPHONSUS LIGUORI: GIVE ME JESUS CHRIST

July 31 and August 1 respectively

As humans we are curious about each other and our unique experiences. The popularity of news programs testifies to this but they do have a tendency to emphasize how one dies over how one lives. St. Alphonus Liguori and St. Ignatius of Loyola are two people whose lives are worth looking at.

St. Alphonsus Liguori lived in Naples, Italy in the 17 to 18 century. He died at the age of ninety-one, and as a historical perspective, that was just after the American Revolution. He was a lawyer by education, but following a career in which he never lost a case until a trial was corrupted politically. Thereafter, he devoted his life to the importance of prayer, with an especial devotion to the Blessed Sacrament and the Virgin Mary. He was as brilliant a theologian as he was a lawyer. His small precious book, *Visits to the Blessed Sacrament*, revolutionized this devotion from then to the present, and it is a wonderful companion to use when attending First Friday adoration. He founded the Redemptorist Congregation.

Alphonsus realized that apart from the abundant graces derived from faith, liturgy, the sacraments and prayer that the most valuable devotion as a Catholic is the Adoration of the Blessed Sacrament. Instead of wondering what to do during that period, his little book helps to structure the time initially as it leads the reader who has just come in from the busy world into the quiet sanctum where God is present. In a meaningful way, with the short meditations that take about ten minutes to read, one can then transition into the unstructured space of kneeling, sitting, talking, or listening to God.

From the very first visit via Alphonsus a shift occurs in the mind and the body—a peaceful, indelible vision of reality descends—a life changing spiritual wind. The phrase from the Gospel of St. Matthew, "Come to me all you who labor and are burdened and I will give you rest," (Matt 11:28) takes on real meaning. Tender mercies of refuge, peace, comfort, and blessings written about by saints are palpable gifts felt by the average person. Alphonsus lovingly reminds us to return to the source of everlasting meaning, life, and love in this timeless devotion.

About two hundred years earlier, St. Ignatius of Loyola was born in Spain. He lived a comfortable aristocratic lifestyle, and served in the military until he became injured. During his recuperation he was confined to a castle with no reading material other than stories of the life of Christ. There in the wilderness of illness, injured and isolated, he entered unknown territory and experienced a conversion. He decided to become a soldier for Christ. He became the founder of the esteemed Jesuit order, originally begun as a missionary sect, and later devoted to the education of youth.

Like Alphonsus, Ignatius is another inestimable intellectual and holy giant who shaped lives for generations to come through his *Spiritual Exercises*, and his influence on education has fashioned the world and American society through its strong academic Catholic colleges and his spiritualism conforming to the love of Jesus.

THE TRANSFIGURATION OF THE LORD AND THE MYSTICAL BODY OF CHRIST: I HAVE GIVEN YOU A MODEL TO FOLLOW SO THAT AS I HAVE DONE FOR YOU, YOU SHOULD ALSO DO (JOHN 13:15)

Understanding the Mystical Body of Christ, like all of the mysteries of our faith, is not something we can achieve. However, for those mysteries to have meaning for us we have to be able to relate to them. One such way is through the unit of the family.

The family is the basic, logical, natural, biological, unit of organization that creates, socializes, supports, and sustains us at least in the ideal. Society and our own individual lives depend upon it. The family is the cornerstone of our lives. Whether a happy group or one we want to forget, or one we long for or want to perpetuate, whether it is functional or dysfunctional, family affects the structure of our life. Just as we share in family life, its joys, sorrows, intimacies and dreams, all families coming together constitute society, and societies of like identity, through culture, make up nations.

Largely due to technology, the world has come together in many ways but it has always reached out to others even in primitive times. We are jointly interrelated economically, politically, socially, and religiously and so we share money, governments, lifestyles, and liturgies. Some aspects of culture like tragedies, sports, art, music, language, and literature connect us and touch our common core. It seems in every culture and nation that we are all looking for the truth that objectifies our own subjective reality thus making our lives more meaningful.

But beyond sympathy, and even empathy, there is the unity that only God can provide. Christ is everywhere—in the good, in the bad, in our families, in our enemies, in those we like, in those we don't like, in our fellow citizens, our parish and in the world. This is what the second commandment that Jesus spoke about means. *Love thy neighbor as ourselves* creates the spirit of the Body of Christ. While the Communion of Saints is made up of the baptized of all eternity who choose God, the Mystical Body of Christ is all of us since the beginning of the world to the end of time, as Jesuit theologian Teilhard de Chardin would call it, "the sap of humanity." It can be sticky!

Our bodies and souls are connected through him for we were created in his image. We are part of his body and our body will be glorified similar to the Transfiguration that James the Greater, John, and Peter beheld. Most of us will not go up onto mountains like Jesus to have our true nature revealed. Even Jesus did that only with his best friends and for a short period in his entire life. But whether we spend a second with a stranger or decades with a spouse we have that same opportunity to show them the glimmer of Christ in our eyes. Resurrection has already happened. It is already a reality. Yes there is death and suffering in life but so is there resurrection. If we live that way—happy, whole, alive and most of all loving—the Mystical Body of Christ will be a reality for the world. We will help save each other through the divine love given to us by him.

THE FEAST OF THE ASSUMPTION OF THE BLESSED VIRGIN MARY INTO HEAVEN: *THEOTOKOS!* MOTHER OF GOD

August 15

As she blends into the blue white dome of heaven, the clouds pave a carpet for her to tread, and the angels escort her into the embrace of her son. With arms folded and eyes uplifted she is as humble and beautiful and pure as the day the angel invited her to become the Mother of God. Only God can make a soul and the God of all eternity who became man in Mary welcomes her to his home as she welcomed him into hers. She has lived her life and fulfilled her destiny as the mother of the Second Person of the Blessed Trinity. Her life has been incomparable—she was the Mother of God, a life of wonder, mystery and joys as incomprehensible as the sorrows that matched them. But earthly life is over and she rises on a mother's hope through her son's love.

Today is the Assumption of the Blessed Virgin Mary into heaven. Mary had died earlier, perhaps forty days earlier. The assumption is either in Jerusalem or Turkey, most likely the former, since all of the apostles are there—well almost. Remember Thomas is running through the hills to get there!

The Assumption actually did not become dogma until 1950. However from the time she died, throughout the early Church and to the present day, this is something the people believed in, a good example of their common sense, and insightfulness of belief and faith-based reason. The belief did not have to be promulgated to be believed. She is God's mother. Could anything less have happened?

Other feasts commemorate Mary—her queenship next week on August 22, her nativity on September 8, her Immaculate Conception on December 8, her manifestation as Our Lady of Guadalupe on December 12, and Our Lady of Lourdes on February 12, and many more. Depending upon which day it falls, the Assumption is a Holy Day of Obligation and the most important feast of Mary. This event is commemorated as the fourth decade of the Glorious Mysteries of the rosary.

Death and suffering will have to come first as they did for Mary, but she can be our partner in it. No one knows better than her how to endure it. But all of this will come to pass. After an abyss of sorrows there will be an abundance of joy. So in the midst of our busy daily life and struggles, take some time to look upward today. Gaze at the comforting blue canopy of the sky and the shimmering clouds that playfully take on the shapes of babies and dragons, angels and sheep. The blue and the white of her dress and mantle are spread before us. It is an assumption skyline and Mary is accessible, beckoning us into pastoral action to do the will of the Lord as she accomplished by her assent to be the mother of Jesus. Look up at the limitless, changing, yet ever-present sky that brings light, water and life—it is a lot like Mary.

SPECIAL TOPIC—INDIAN MARKET AND THE NATIVE AMERICAN LITURGY: ALL IS FASHIONED BY YOUR HAND*

In New Mexico, parishioners are blessed to have the arts indigenous to that area celebrated in the Indian and Spanish markets where people from all over the world gather to honor their inspired artisans. This week is the largest of all events in Santa Fe, Indian Market weekend. The cultural aspects of the weekend are played out on the plaza in the booths replete with contemporary and traditional Indian arts of world class and museum quality. Dances, food, costumes, and all aspects of the culture come together to celebrate the fruits of the earth, and the artistic imagination of the craftsmen. Awards will be competed for and attained in acknowledgement of the artists' skills. The sweat of long days and nights, the toil of arthritic hands and tired imaginations, the initial resistance of the materials, and the pressures of competition, are replenished by the joy of physically creating something of beauty, objects of wonder.

Inside, the basilica looks different from any other time of year. It is summer; maybe what we could truly call Indian summer, that is summer at its zenith. The Altar Society has bundled the pine with the corn, sunflowers and cattails, the lavender, native grasses, and willowy aspens. The flowers are at their fullest, smiling in satisfaction that they are gathered and displayed. The birth of these plants may have been painful—seedlings searching for soil, saplings thirsting for rain, fruits longing to give taste, and gourds gathering sunshine. Birth can be painful but it is the process that gives life. Their oranges, yellows, reds and purples shout, "I am alive now." No plant or flower is unliturgical. They are God's entire making. "All creation lives to hold you." **

Overhead the energy of the universe gathers in the cumulus clouds and the rumbling thunder. Lightning says, "Love me!" Breezes pass by. Who knows where they begin or end as they are captured for a moment in a clay vase or a bird's feather? The sun shines outward, its rays never reflecting back on itself. It skates on silver jewelry or the emotional lines of a bronze sculpture. The liturgy of song, dance, drums, and worship is the union of our shared and diverse connection as Catholics. The proud buffalo dancing in front of the altar at the Native American Liturgy (Mass) humbly lowers his eyes in the presence of God, and the slope of the eagles' wings points to him. It is the nature of love.

Soon it will be Labor Day, the "official" end of summer and all its playfulness. This weekend no matter where we are, let us silently marvel at the nature of God in his people and his creation, the sensory experience of the beauty of the natural and the material world, and what they have to tell us about life. Smell the roasted corn, the pungent chile, the fragrant cedar and lavender. Admire and thank an artist for their expression. Give thanks to our God of plenty for the richness of life and the pain that gives rise to it.

*Hymn. Haugen, Marty. *Song at the Center*. Chicago: G.I.A. Publications, Inc. 1993.

**Hymn. Farrell, Bernadette. *God Beyond All Names*. OCP, 1990.

THE FEASTS OF ST. MONICA AND ST. AUGUSTINE: THE PATH IS NOT LONG FROM YOUR HEART TO GOD (ST. AUGUSTINE)

AUGUST 27 AND 28 RESPECTIVELY

Perhaps the most recognized of mother and son saints are St. Monica and her son, St. Augustine, Bishop of Hippo. Born in the fourth century AD in northern Africa, Augustine was a brilliant but wayward son who wanted to experience everything in the hope of understanding truth. Much to the sadness of his mother, a pious and charitable woman, Monica suffered this disappointment along with the difficulties of life with her husband. As mothers and wives are known to be, she was patient and even zealous in the concern for her family, and slowly one by one they returned to God. One year before his death, her husband was baptized into the church, and Augustine followed as his great intellect, the prayers of his mother, and the will of God brought him to that truth he sought. Once he found God he never strayed. In Milan, Italy St. Ambrose baptized him as an adult thus beginning his formidable Catholic profession.

Augustine made quick strides in sanctity and the church hierarchy due to his education and hunger for God, and he spent most of his religious career defending the church in the numerous heresies that characterized his time. As a Doctor of the Church, he is most known for his doctrine of the Trinity whom he saw as the lover, the loved, and the love, a beautiful image referring to the father, son, and Holy Spirit respectively. His book, *The Confessions,* details his dissolute life that eventually lead to God, and it is moving to read his heartfelt and poetic images.

Monica and Augustine's relationship are akin to that of St. Helena and her son St. Constantine. Both mothers were mistreated by their spouses and both sons were unpracticing Christians who then became saints. Constantine, the emperor of Rome, was born about eighty years before Augustine. At that time Christian persecution was thriving. In a battle, in 313 AD, Constantine saw the sign of the cross in the sky and heard the words "Conquer by this." He then allowed and established the Christianization of the Roman Empire through the Edict of Milan, which guaranteed religious tolerance to all. Although he was baptized on his deathbed, he did great things for his country and the church. His mother St. Helena went to Jerusalem and found the true cross although her true cross was certainly the sorrow she carried like Monica.

Both Augustine and Constantine were intellectual and political geniuses who made a mark on their time and the future of the church. Monica and Helena, women of reflection like Mary, give all parents who suffer their children's rejection of their inherited faith the hope that through the gifts of education, example, free will, and prayer all things are possible with God. The nature of a gift is to pass it from hand to hand, and the nature of hope is the love of parents and those who give.

THE FEAST OF THE NATIVITY OF THE BLESSED VIRGIN MARY AND THE FEAST OF THE HOLY NAME OF MARY: HAIL MARY, FULL OF GRACE, THE LORD IS WITH THEE

SEPTEMBER 8 AND THE FIRST SUNDAY AFTER HER NATIVITY RESPECTIVELY

This week, two feasts commemorate the Blessed Virgin Mary—the feast of her nativity, and the feast of her holy name. It seems fitting to anticipate the beginning of the liturgical year at Advent in a few months with remembering Mary's central role in salvation history and how focal she should be in our lives as well.

The nativity or birthday of Mary is probably a day we don't think about much, yet her birthday was of course requisite for the birth of Jesus. Remember, as she told Bernadette at Lourdes in language not quite understandable in the vernacular of the time, "I am the Immaculate Conception." Here she is telling us that it was she who was conceived immaculately, meaning without original sin, through Ann and Jacob as her parents. She is unparalleled in her bodily and spiritual purity, making her fit to be the Mother of God.

Mary is so inextricably linked to our faith that perhaps we don't think of the etymology of her name, yet it sheds some light on our understanding of her. "Mary," derived from perhaps Egyptian or Hebrew, means, "sea of sorrow," "sea of bitterness," "wished for child," "beloved," and "beautiful,"—surely proper appellations.

Mary, as the mother of the incarnate God and the church, has many names bespeaking her vital relation to us individually, culturally, and collectively. As Blessed, Holy, Queen, Immaculate, Mother, Mediatrix, Virgin, Tower, Refuge, Hope, and Lady, and hundreds of other titles we can invoke and celebrate her for the many apparitions she has made to so many cultures and peoples, and in the numerous roles she assumes for us.

The minor Feast of the Holy Name of Mary, celebrated during the octave of the Nativity of Mary, is perhaps another forgotten day. We think of the Holy Name of Jesus and honor it in song, the names of churches, our bowed heads at the mention of his name, and by not taking his name in vain. Mary's name is similar, also reflected in the names of hymns and churches and also not to be taken lightly by dishonoring it in our speech. Saints claim, the devil flees when he hears her name, so powerful is the name of Mary. When we call on her she is at our side.

So this week, as we celebrate her birthday and her holy name, let us give thanks for her advent in the world and her loving presence by reflecting on her various names. May we keep her in our lives every day of the year so that when we meet her in heaven we will be able to say that her holy name was the gate to God just as she was the gate, the new ark of the covenant, housing and bringing into our lives Jesus, our Lord and Savior. She is Mary.

THE FEAST OF THE EXALTATION OF THE HOLY CROSS: BEHOLD THE WOOD OF THE CROSS*

SEPTEMBER 14

We are Catholics and the sign of our faith is the sign of the cross. As we know in Christ's time, the cross was a sign of ignominy and defeat, and crucifixion a common Roman method by which criminals were punished and killed. It wasn't a beautiful jewelry symbol, or a mark by which one wanted to identify oneself. However, as an archetypal character found in many cultures, its primal, opposite, intersecting strokes created a support both for crucifixion as well as for pointing the way through life to heaven.

Over time, the way in which Christ was sacrificed for our sins was represented in cultural and religious art and literature and has become the mark of our faith. We honor the cross in our churches, our liturgy, when we pray, in our homes, in our jewelry and art, and by making the sign of the cross with holy water when we enter and leave a church.

Amidst so many crosses used for convicts and rebels, St. Helena, a convert to Christianity at the age of sixty-three and the mother of the Emperor Constantine the Great, sought out the true cross. In the third century, at the age of over 80, she travelled to Palestine and oversaw its excavation, close to Calvary, along with two other crosses. She had part of it brought it back to Rome where it is revered in Santa Croce in

Gerusalemme, the Church of the Holy Cross, in the Chapel of the Holy Relics, which was once her residence.

Visiting that basilica in Rome I stood with my husband in that chapel where there are also two thorns from Christ's crown, a nail used to pierce him, and parts of the sign over his head that identified him as Jesus of Nazareth, along with pieces of the good thief's cross. In silence, in the corner of the chapel sat a solitary monk, his body bent forward, his hands holding his face, as if in grief at the foot of the cross. He seemed agonized to be the sentinel of the relics of God's suffering and death. I was moved to think that my patron Saint Helena had been where I now stood almost two thousand years later, and that she had brought some of the cross back to Rome just like the cross had been brought into my life.

The cross has so much significance for us, we can never hear enough about it, and we all have, I am sure, a personal relationship with it that largely deals with suffering but also joy. It is a sacred marker, a directional pointing the way up to God and across to each other through him. Everything else is on the side.

St. Thomas Aquinas, Doctor of the Church and author of the some of the most complete Catholic theological works, said when asked where he learned so much, simply pointed to the crucifix. Let it teach us the way too.

> *Prayer of St. Thomas Aquinas Before a Crucifix*
>
> Grant me the grace, o merciful God, to desire ardently all that is pleasing to thee, to examine it prudently, to acknowledge it truthfully, and to accomplish it perfectly for the praise and glory of thy name. Amen

*Hymn. *Behold the Wood*. Schutte, Daniel L. OCP, 1976.

THE FEAST OF ST. VINCENT DE PAUL: CARE FOR EACH OTHER, I HAVE CARED FOR YOU*

September 27

As Catholics, we are familiar with the name of St. Vincent de Paul. Our parishes may have a St. Vincent de Paul Society or a St. Vincent de Paul thrift shop, or our community a hospital named after him. His name is synonymous with charity, but who was he and what did he do to become so revered?

Not unlike celebrated saints or us, Vincent de Paul aspired to a comfortable life. Born in the late 1500s, he lived at a time when despair as much as the plague was infecting Europe. As people isolated themselves and ignored their neighbors and friends, Vincent de Paul, a privileged priest in France, encouraged the people to care for each other. He had an especial devotion to the poor peasants, the imprisoned, and even the slaves who worked in the ship galleys.

Monsieur Vincent's devotion to the poor inspired many who responded, especially devout and wealthy women. Soup kitchens were established, and food and clothing distributed to the poor. His charitable ideas spread as quickly as the plague to many chapters and countries. He became quite popular with the court, but he longed for the simplicity of doing work for the poor personally, not just through his societies which sometimes got caught up in the trappings of an organization. Personal service to the poor he saw as intrinsic to Christ-like service. He founded the Congregation of the Mission, a religious order of priests, to stabilize and continue the work begun in different places, as well as the Daughters and Missionaries of Charity, who worked in the hospitals of France.

Relatively soon after his death he was canonized. As an unsurpassed benefactor to the poor, his exemplary action and principle of relief spread to almost every country in the world in the lay organization of the St. Vincent de Paul Society, and the religious order he founded, and others he inspired. Popes have created indulgences for those who aid the society through alms and money, but personal service in the form of corporal and spiritual works of mercy** is a hallmark of his legacy.

Many churches have collections allocated to the St. Vincent de Paul Society. The society in turn gives it to numerous and diverse groups in the community. St. Vincent de Paul was truly an extraordinary man who served everyman, as did our Lord, offering hope in the form of comfort to strangers and the ordinary people that we all are.

> **Corporal works of mercy: feed the hungry, give drink to the thirsty, clothe the naked, shelter the homeless, visit the sick, visit those in prison, and bury the dead.
>
> Spiritual works of mercy: instruct the ignorant, counsel the doubtful, admonish the sinner, comfort the sorrowful, forgive injuries, bear wrongs patiently, pray for the living and the dead.
>
> *Hymn. *Love One Another.* Dufford S. J., Robert. Text based on John 13:34–35 and 1 Corinthians 13. OCP, 1987.

THE FEAST OF THE ARCHANGELS: BEHOLD THE ANGEL OF THE LORD

September 29

There is an invisible world, a world as unseen and as real as the wind or love. It is the world that existed before man, the world of heavenly angels, non-corporeal beings close to God, who ministered to him in heaven, and in Jesus' earthly journey. They appeared to prophets, Mary, Joseph and the saints, and guard us in our daily lives. The *Catechism of the Catholic Church* (#328) says this is a truth of our faith.

Angel means messenger. Nine choirs of angels were created. Some announced Jesus's birth, adored him in the manger, ministered to him in the desert, beheld him at the foot of the cross, and will come with him at the end of time. They adorn churches and holy cards. We sing about them at Christmas in hymns and carols. Even non-religious people like angels; they are pretty and powerful. But what role do they have in modern-day life?

We think about the angels especially when we are children; they are our friends. The archangels preside over the throngs of angels and have figured largely in salvation history. The Roman Catholic Church recognizes three archangels who are also given the honorific versus the canonized title of saint. They are the messengers and servants of God: Saints Michael, Gabriel, and Raphael.

Michael, the angelic warrior, is the defender and protector of the good, and healer of the sick. He has made numerous apparitions throughout history, aiding in battles and carrying the deceased to heaven. St. Michael is the chief archangel, his name a question asking, "Who is like God?" He and his legions cast out Lucifer from heaven when Lucifer in his envy could not accept that God created man in his image and likeness. Thus the angels of pure spirit and intelligence were banished from heaven and the primordial battle of good versus evil began. Michael is the patron saint of policemen, emergency workers, mariners, and patron of battles.

Gabriel's name means, "My master is God." He is the great messenger, announcing the birth of St. John the Baptist and appearing to Mary with the news that she was chosen to be the mother of the Savior. He appeared to Moses and David, and is the angel of the book of Revelation, who will blow the trumpet at the end of time. He is the patron saint of radio and television.

Raphael's name means, "It is God who heals." He is recounted in the Old Testament book of Tobit, disguised in human form as a traveling companion of Tobias. He is depicted with a fish, because he used the gall bladder bile of the fish he caught to heal the blindness of the elder Tobias. He is the patron saint of medical workers and matchmakers.

We may be more interested in the saints than the angels because we can relate more to the human saints, but angels surround and serve God and us constantly. One is always right next to us, guiding and protecting us in ways we don't understand. We need their healing, to make room for them, and to pay heed to their messages.

St. Francis de Sales says of the angels, "Make yourself familiar with the angels, and behold them frequently in spirit, for without being seen, they are present with you."

Statue of St. Francis of Assisi in front of the Cathedral Basilica of St. Francis of Assisi, Sante Fe, New Mexico, decorated for his feast day

THE FEAST OF ST. FRANCIS OF ASSISI: THE JOY OF HOLY POVERTY

OCTOBER 4

Born in a cattle stall not unlike our Lord, and buried as he requested on the Hill of Hell, a burial place for criminals much like Golgotha was a place for executions, the great Saint Francis of Assisi has been called the mirror of the world. In a time which seemed to be the time of most history and not unlike our own, a time of political, economic, social, spiritual and ecclesiastical unrest, instead of criticizing those institutions, Francis chose action in the form of Gospel values to help his fellow man and their ills.

To Francis, the nativity of the Lord as well as his crucifixion, were the major events that shape our lives, and so he celebrated them in the form of creating the first nativity scenes for catechetical purposes. Replacing Lucifer as the light of the world in heaven, he had the beautiful view of the solidarity of man, God, and nature. The material, natural world of creation was the sister to the spiritual eden of heaven, a place to be enjoyed, cared for, and united with.

So great was his understanding of God in the world that the animals loved him, the angels surrounded him, he received visions of the crucifix as central to salvation, heard the voice of God, and understood the heart of Mary. In his humility, he chose to remain a deacon over a priest. He humbled and edified popes with his poverty of body, mind, and spirit. His worn tunic, mended with sackcloth, was good enough for this life.

So great is St. Francis in his holiness that we can only contemplate the obvious—his love of God and the world. He was the first of about three hundred saints to receive the stigmata, the sacred wounds suffered by Christ in his crucifixion. Can you imagine the holiness he had to be the first to receive and suffer these holy wounds, wounds he hid from the sight of others for several years, and which caused him much pain? When he died, it is said that the friars who tended to him saw his soul lift as a star to heaven, the bells of the nearby church, St. Stephen Martyr, peeled spontaneously, and a flock of chirping skylarks circled overhead.

Even though Francis is the patron of many churches, and tomes of material have been written about him, and religious ordained and non-ordained orders are deeply devoted to his spirituality, as an average person, how do we understand Francis today? In essence, Francis took the time and experienced the joy of seeing God in everyone and everything. By his holy poverty of spirit, he was freed from the material world and made heir to everything that God is in creation and in us.

On many levels we are a long way from his birthplace of Assisi, Italy. But if we want to see Assisi, all we have to do is care for the natural world, the communal world of each other, and the loving world of God thus engendering peace over violence. This was the joyful task of St. Francis. It can be found in our church, our world, and our hearts for all time. It is called love.

Gubio, the wolf Francis befriended

THE FEAST OF OUR LADY OF THE MOST HOLY ROSARY: PREACH MY ROSARY

OCTOBER 7

Rosary beads. How many have we owned in our lives? Rosaries of wood, crystal, plastic, pearls, seeds, gems, glass, silver, gold, cloisonné, and even flowers. Rosary beads of every color, size, and shape. Rosaries from different shrines and places. We may have a favorite rosary, or may be still looking for the perfect one. Rosaries are said for every occasion: celebrations, funerals, processions, right to life, and for daily strength. It is said at home, in cars, in churches, and in stadiums, with others, or in our privacy.

Revealed to St. Dominic in 1208 as a devotion pleasing to Mary, and further restored to practice in the 1400s by Blessed Alan de la Roche, the rosary is a most beautiful prayer. It is a powerful contemplative meditation that takes about twenty minutes to say, but has the enduring ability to center and anchor us in the realities of our personal and collective day. As we recite the four categories of mysteries that the rosary honors—the Joyful, Sorrowful, Glorious and Luminous Mysteries—on different days of the week that are the assigned to them—we travel with Jesus through Mary in a circle of unbroken praise that is called the rosary.

At Fatima, Mary told the children how important this prayer was for one individually as well as collectively for the conversion of nations, and the establishment of international peace. She revealed to St. Lucia dos Santos, the elder of the Fatima children, "There is no problem, I tell you, that we cannot resolve by the prayer of the Holy Rosary." If we believe that, it seems we should be praying the rosary frequently.

In mideastern counties at the sound of the bell five times a day, many stop and prostrate themselves and pray to God and to reorient one's life. For a people who are always on the go like us, this is a very moving experience to witness. That interval probably adds up to the time it would take to say a rosary. If we could all do that everyday our over-stimulated lives would gain the added balance and inner strength to be involved in the busy, stressful, demanding world of our culture never mind the glory it would give to Jesus and Mary, and the intentions it would satisfy.

But of course it is not about the new or worn beads that form a garland in our smooth or wrinkled hands. Regardless of the beads or the day of week, the most pleasing rosary is the one that is said from the heart. It is not one said monotonously or proudly, or with eyes closed disengaged from reality, for like the beads, we are all connected to each other. It needs to be said with the fullness of consciousness of genuine prayer that unites us with each other when we make our behavior consonant with love.

Mary said the rosary is a crown of roses. It is a gesture of love, with Mary as the route that begins and ends with God. The best way to understand the rosary is to pray the rosary. Give Mary a crown of roses daily. As Mary urged, "Preach my rosary."

THE FEAST OF ST. LUKE THE EVANGELIST: LUKE IS THE ONLY ONE WITH ME (2 TIM 3:11)

OCTOBER 18

St. Luke is the author of two great canonical works, his Gospel and the Acts of the Apostles. St. Luke was born a Gentile and a Greek, and became a doctor by profession and a disciple of the apostles. He was a companion to St. Paul, and ministered to Paul physically for his ailments, and spiritually as his companion when Paul was imprisoned in Rome for two years prior to his beheading. He never knew Jesus directly.

Each evangelist has a perspective presented in the Gospel as a function of who they are and their relationship to Jesus. While there are similar topics found in all the Gospels such as the Baptism of Jesus, there are also thematic divergences along with the obvious stylistic differences. The Gospel of Luke, written in a poetic and literary style, interspersed with medical language, is unique in its attention to the many miracles and healings of Jesus, his attention to the poor and the ill, his regard for women, and his knowledge of the political times, geography, history, and travel. His recounting of certain historical events constitutes for us today what we call the Joyful Mysteries of the rosary. His Gospel is also the only one to contain the most complete nativity story, Mary's prayer-filled greeting to Elizabeth that we call the Magnificat, the tale of the prodigal son, and the story of Lazarus raised from the dead. Imagine our faith without such rich and eloquent stories!

The Gospels rotate in the liturgical years, and every three years the Gospel of Luke is read at Mass as Year C. It appears in the readings at Mass at Advent and goes through to the end of the liturgical year. But the beauty of Luke's Gospel lingers beyond the liturgical year and we can read it any time in our Bible or missal. Read it at Christmas or when you want to be reacquainted with the father, the brother, and the wayward but repentant son in the parable of the prodigal son, certainly roles we have all had the opportunity to imitate or reflect upon.

Perhaps the most moving experience of my recent trip to Italy was to stand in the small, cold, dark, stone prison where Saints Peter and Paul were enchained in Rome, awaiting their crucifixion or beheading respectively. It is comforting to think that Luke as a true physician and Christian was there, for as Paul said when all had abandoned him, it was Luke who remained with him to the end, his "most dear physician." "Only Luke is with me," he wrote.

The lessons of Luke are many. While everyone is not a physician, we can all be the healer to others that he was to Paul, the healer he painted Jesus to be in his Gospel. In today's world there are many ways to heal although it is not easy. We can be the caregiver to a weak and aging parent, spouse or family member, a task that breaks one's heart as we share and observe their fragility and decline. We can be the parent to a sick and helpless child, or a visiting nurse to those we don't even know like the sick in hospitals, hospice or in their home. We can bring them the Eucharist as a friend. Even by being more understanding of anyone's illness, through a kind inquiry, a card or an e-mail, or prayer, we can give hope and comfort. To read from the great St. Paul that only Luke was with him at the end is a startling thought, but it is also hopeful for us that maybe we can be the one person that we were meant to be and like Luke, minister with healing kindness until the promise of the resurrection is fulfilled. Let Luke be with us as he was with Paul.

THE FEAST OF ST. PAUL OF THE CROSS: MAY THE PASSION OF JESUS CHRIST BE ALWAYS IN OUR HEARTS*

OCTOBER 19

Mystics have been part of many cultures for a large part of history. The Roman Catholic Church has been blessed and has nurtured many mystics in her relatively short history. Both men and women from different countries, as mystics in the church tradition, have received a revelation or a direct relationship with God that has given them a union of their soul with his divinity. St. Paul of the Cross sits on par with St. Thomas

Aquinas, St. Faustina, St. Catherine of Siena, St. Teresa of Avila, St. Pio, St. John of the Cross and many others, and shares with them the common denominator of the contemplation and passionate understanding of the central redemptive reality of our faith, the cross.

Born in the late 1600s in Italy, Paolo Francesco Danei was a devout young man profoundly influenced by the writings on the love of God by the great St. Frances de Sales of France. He had an especial devotion to the Blessed Sacrament and called the crucifix his book and the crucified his model. He was deeply impressed by the gratuitous gift of Jesus' sacrifice on the cross, and had visions and heard voices in this regard to form a religious community devoted to Jesus' passion. Thus, the order of the Passionist priests was formed of which he served humbly and reluctantly as superior general until his death. The congregation was marked by their dedication to contemplation, solitude, and prayer, that they continue to this day, based on St. John's life of austerity and his union with the cross.

Currently the Passionist order consists of over two thousand ordained men and several thousand religious women and lay people who serve in many countries throughout the world. The symbol that adorns their simple attire is the heart of Christ with three nails at its base and a cross on the top. Their motto is, "May the passion of Christ always be in our hearts." This phrase guides their apostolic work with the poor, the displaced, the ill, the suffering, and all the least of one's brethren with whom Christ identified himself. St. Paul of the Cross died on the feast of St. Luke, October 18, and is buried in the Basilica of Saints John and Paul in Rome.

*Passionists' motto

THE FEAST OF ALL SAINTS AND ALL SOULS DAY: THE COMMUNION OF SAINTS, THE FORGIVENESS OF SINS

November 1 and 2 respectively

One of our Holy Days of Obligation, All Saints Day, crowns the fall. It is a joyful day that commemorates all the faithful who have become saints and are now with God in heaven. Throughout much of church history, All Saints Day was celebrated anytime between the first Friday after Easter to Pentecost, but was then moved to its current date of November 1.

Originally it celebrated just the death of martyred saints, and then confessors, but now encompasses all the saints collectively as a union, and because they are too numerous to have a separate feast day.

There are so many wonderful saints to emulate and honor as models, including our patron saints, the saints of the past, the newly canonized saints, and saints of every country. Each is so special individually; imagine them all together in their solidarity! We commemorate them in parts of the Mass, sing about them in the moving *Litany of the Saints*, and get to know them better by reading books about their lives.

The following day, November 2, is All Souls Day. It is a more somber celebration also stemming from ancient times in the church. It remembers the deceased who are not yet with God but are being purified in purgatory. Prayers by the living can release them from that suffering. We all have relatives and friends, associates and acquaintances that have died and whom we think about especially on that day. It is common church custom to write their names on a slip of paper that is kept on the altar in prayer for the month of November. But what about all those who die with no one—on the streets, alone in hospitals and nursing homes, in natural disasters and wars, those who have never heard the word of God? Surely we should pray for them too at least as much as for those we know, maybe even more so.

These two feasts are celebrated back to back and it makes sense because they are interrelated. At the end of time the saints and those who are awaiting the beatific vision will attain it through the mercy of God. But in the meantime the saints in heaven, those in purgatory, and we on earth who do not reject Jesus constitute a special union called the Communion of Saints. It is a fellowship, united as the Mystical Body of Christ, with him as our head. It is the church.

Are saints born or bred? Do they choose sainthood or are they given that gift from God? Ultimately everything comes from God including our free will to choose goodness. We can choose to accept the invitation be a saint for holiness is our calling. St. Benedict said, "Let nothing be preferred to the work of God." The work of God is for us to become a saint by love of God in action. We can begin that by praying for those separated from us, and praising those in heaven, until we reunite someday as the Communion of Saints in eternity.

DEDICATION OF THE BASILICA OF ST. JOHN LATERAN: OUR MOTHER CHURCH

NOVEMBER 9

Contrary to popular thought, it is not the great St. Peter's Basilica in Rome that is the mother church of Catholicism, but the Archbasilica of the Most Holy Savior, St. John the Baptist and St. John the Evangelist at the Lateran, more commonly known as the Basilica of St. John Lateran. St. John Lateran is the chief of the four major Basilicas of Rome, along with St. Peter's, St. Mary Major, and St. Paul Outside the Wall.

The church partially derives its name, "Lateran" from the property it is built on, the palace of the Laterani family near the walls of Rome. In the tenth century the church was dedicated to St. John the Baptist, and in the twelfth century to St. John the Evangelist, Gospel writer. Prior to that is was dedicated to Our Most Holy Savior.

The basilica is the pope's church and it is here that the papal throne is installed. The church itself has a rather regal style since it was originally a palace, then given to the popes by Constantine the Great, son of St. Helena, who brought remnants of the Holy Cross back to Rome.

Apart from a place of worship the basilica houses many extraordinary relics. Within the basilica are the Holy Steps, wooden stairs encasing the white marble ones said to have been those that Jesus walked to meet Pontius Pilate at the start of his passion when he was condemned to death. Its beautiful baptistry was once the only place for one to be baptized for many generations in Rome. The High Altar, used only by Popes, is said to contain the cedar table that St. Peter used to celebrate Mass. What a vision!

Like all churches in Rome, St. John Lateran is a beautiful historical church that is unique in that it is the pope's, the Bishop of Rome's church, but also the church of the people of God that is part of our universal Catholic heritage, and it is wonderful to behold and to appreciate its unique treasures.

St. Augustine reminds us in referring to the walls and the timber and the stone that go into the formidable construction of any church that "they do not make a house for the Lord until they are fitted together with love." We too can build the church by loving it into being, and sustaining it with love in our own parishes, as it is today and has been for centuries at the Basilica of St. John Lateran.

DEDICATION OF THE BASILICAS OF SAINTS PETER AND PAUL: CALLED TO BE APOSTLES BY JESUS CHRIST

NOVEMBER 18

Saints Peter and Paul, contemporaries and apostles, martyrs and pillars of the church, are the patron saints of Rome and our greatest saints. Churches throughout the world are named after them; in particular two of the four principle churches in Rome that are our legacy—the Basilica of St. Paul Outside the Wall, St. Peter's Basilica, St. John Lateran, and St. Mary Major.

The Basilica of St. Paul Outside the Wall is so named because it sits on the immediate outskirts of the city of Rome, which was encircled by a wall as many ancient cities were. It is an impressive basilica, with an equally imposing statue of St. Paul in front of it that conveys the religious stature and power of Paul. It is here that the chains that held St. Paul can be seen, as moving as the chains that held St. Peter, enshrined at the Church of St. Peter in Chains. It is here that Saint Paul was beheaded, and it is said that his head rolled three times and three springs sprung from the earth. Whether this is mythological or historical, the story reflects the sanctity and mystery of Paul.

St. Peter's Basilica, of all the churches in the world, certainly has the reputation of being the greatest Catholic Church, although St. John Lateran is our mother church. St. Peter's is unsurpassed in the volume of religious art that it houses, its size, statues, crypts, chapels, history, how long it took to be constructed, the number of artists who worked on it, the number of popes buried there, and the number of visitors to it per year. Its Adoration Chapel reserved for prayer only, is a quiet sanctuary ablaze with the Exposition of the Blessed Sacrament, and electrified with palpable holiness, in contrast to the reverent stir, despite whispering, created by the throngs of visitors in the basilica.

Built on a red rock that was believed to be the original grave of St. Peter, his tomb is revered below the high altar. The juxtaposition of the humble life of the fisherman from Galilee, and the magnificence of St. Peter's, gives testimony to the world of the power of Catholicism, the truth that it incarnates, and the fidelity and depth of the faith of her followers. The hope of Peter is that even if we fail and deny our master, question him and stumble, we too can be saved and called to holiness and witness to Jesus. Like Paul we may have persecuted others, and we may need the drama of being "knocked off our horse" to make us return to him. It may take us being blinded like Paul to be able to see Jesus all around us.

Peter and Paul, perfect in their imperfection, first and foremost saints, fisherman turned pope and persecutor turned prolific and powerful writer, together in Rome, heading our repertoire of saints. Crucified and beheaded, entrusted with the keys of the kingdom of heaven and the conversion of nations. We give honor to them and their churches.

THE FEAST OF CHRIST THE KING: AND HIS KINGDOM WILL HAVE NO END

It is the last Sunday of the liturgical year, the Feast of Christ the King. A new liturgical year begins next week with Advent, and from then on we journey with Jesus from his humble and incomprehensible entrance into the world at Christmas, and a brief respite in Ordinary Time, through Lent, Easter and the post-Easter feasts of the Ascension and Pentecost. Then the longest period of the liturgical year sets in, the beautiful, rhythmicity of Ordinary Time. It is an interval replete with Ordinations, weddings, celebrations and yes, even funerals as apparent antitheses of the earthly, temporal union with a partner, to the eternal, spiritual union with Christ. So it is befitting that the Feast of Christ the King crowns the culmination of the church calendar.

Christ is the King of the world. Do we understand that reality, what it means for us now and forever? Have we spent as much time thinking about Christ as king as we have about the presidential election or the financial crisis? Yes, these are serious realities that deeply affect our lives and in some ways our very survival, and they are important institutional vehicles for living out our faith and obtaining a just social order, yet more so does our relationship with Christ. If we acknowledge him as king of our lives, he will surely take care of his people. His kingdom of rich graces will not crash or need a bail out, but will always sustain us. He will not distort truth or sell us out. His kingdom is real and will last forever. His is neither a physical kingdom nor one limited to any one people in time or space, young or old, black or white, rich or poor, male or female. His kingdom is universal.

Scripture compares the kingdom of heaven to a treasure hidden in a field. The man went and sold all that he had to buy that field. It is like a mustard seed, the smallest of seeds that was planted and grew to be a tree that the birds of the air perched upon. It is a net cast out to sea that gathered all types of fish. It is like a man who finds a pearl of great price and sells all that he has to buy that field. The kingdom is like these things and more. It is something worth procuring; it will last forever. Jesus is the king, inheriting the throne of David as the last and eternal king. "But seek first the kingdom [of God] and his righteousness, and all these things will be given you besides" (Matt 6:33).

When he was on earth, we crowned him with thorns. What do we crown him with in our lives today? On this Feast of Christ the King, let us remember who and what is real. We have a king in our lives. *Soli Deo*, only God. "O daughter of Jerusalem! Behold your king is coming to you" (John 12:15). Next week is the first week of Advent. Are we ready for the kingdom? How far will we go to obtain it?

Glossary

ambo—the stand where the readings and the Gospel are read (also referred to as the pulpit)

ambry—the place where the holy oils are stored

apocryphal gospels—works that presented themselves as "authentic" but that did not obtain general acceptance from within the church

candidates—those baptized in another faith who are entering the Roman Catholic Church

canonical gospels—the Gospels of Matthew, Mark, Luke, and John

catechumens—those who take their final steps towards the sacrament of Baptism, and are then confirmed, and receive Holy Eucharist

chrism—oils made of olive oil and balsam that is used sacramentally to confer grace in three of the seven sacraments—Baptism, Confirmation, and Holy Orders

confirmandi—those baptized in the Roman Catholic Church who are confirmed at the Easter Vigil

corporal works of mercy—the actions that feed the hungry, give drink to the thirsty, clothe the naked, shelter the homeless, visit the sick, visit those in prison, and bury the dead

elect—referring to the catechumens after they have undergone the Rite of Election

dayenu—Greek word for abundance

leitourgia—Greek word for the work of the people

manna—nutritious nectar-like food provided by God to the Israelites in their forty years in the desert

ordo—the small book of liturgical options for the church in a particular liturgical year

partial indulgence—a partial remission of temporal punishment due for sins, which have already been forgiven

plenary indulgence—a full remission of temporal punishment due for sins that have already been forgiven. The church grants the indulgence after the sinner has confessed and received absolution

sensor plenius—the full meaning of an Old Testament passage in light of New Testament material

solemnity—a principal holy day commemorating an event in the life of Jesus, Mary, or the saints

spiritual works of mercy—the actions that instruct the ignorant, counsel the doubtful, admonish the sinner, comfort the sorrowful, forgive injuries, bear wrongs patiently, and pray for the living and the dead

synoptic gospels—these are the gospels of Matthew, Mark and Luke. They share similar incidents, teachings, and even much language

Subject/Name Index

Numbers in *italics* indicate images.

Abraham, God's relationship with, 25
abstinence, 48, 80
abundance, 27, 63
actualization, 4
addictions, 59
adoration, Advent and, 8–9
Adoration of the Blessed Sacrament, 115, 125
Advent, 2
    Abraham and, 26
    adoration during, 8–9
    anticipation of, 6–7
    arrival of, 11
    banner for, *13*
    beginning with awareness, 3–4
    Exodus and, 28
    Genesis and, 24
    John the Baptist and, 14
    Lent and, 68
    liturgical environment for, 2–3
    Mary in, 5–6
    Old Testament and, 22
    taking confession during, 16
    themes of, 17
    as time of *dayenu*, 27–28
    as time for deepening appreciation for the Advent wreath, *1*, *2*
    as time for preparation, 17
Alacoque, Margaret Mary, Saint, 38
Alan de la Roche, 139
al-Kamil, Malik, 84
All Saints Day, 142–43
All Souls Day, 143
almsgiving, 48, 49, 62–63, 69, 77
ambry, 65
angels, 135

Annunciation, 68–69
anointing, 64, 65
Anselm, 105
archangels, 135–36
Ark of the Covenant, 8–9
Ascension Thursday, 110–11
ashes, 50
Ash Wednesday, 39, 48, 49–52
Assumption, 127–28
Augustine, Saint, 130–31, 144

Baptism, 15–16, 39, 60–62, 65
    affecting the rest of life, 41
    common belief in, 40
    focus on, during Lent, 39–40
    vows of, 43, 61
baptismal font, 61–62
    at Christmas, *12*
    central as central focus of liturgical journey during Lent, 54
    in Lent, *47*
    in Ordinary Time, *113*
Barbarossa, Frederick, 37
Basilica of St. Francis of Assisi, Italy, *75*, *76*
Basilica of St. John Lateran, 144
Basilica of St. Paul Outside the Wall, 145
Benedict XVI, 53, 63, 106
Benedict of Nursia, Saint, xix, 46, 116, 120–21, 122, 143
benediction, 45
Bible study, 56
Blessed Sacrament chapel, 74
body, resurrection of, 50
Bonaventure, Saint, 123
Bridget of Sweden, Saint, 46

candidates, 60
Candlemas day, 43
Canticle of the Creatures (Francis of Assisi), 83
Caravaggio, 120
Catechism of the Catholic Church, The, xviii
catechumens, 60
Catherine of Siena, Saint, 46, 142
Catholic imagination, xvii, xix
Catholicism, uniqueness of, 38
celibacy, 116
Chrism Mass, 64, 65–66
Chrism oil, 65
Christ. *See also* Jesus
    as king of the world, 146
    resurrection of, 87
    sacrifice of, depicted, *72*, 132
Christmas, 11–12, 87
    approach of, 6
    candle wreath flowers for, *21*
    color for, 10
    cultural emphasis on, 5
    excitement of, 10
    salvation and, 10
    stress of, 4
Church of the Holy Cross, 132–33
church, slow to change, 98
Circumcision of Jesus, 36
Clare, Saint (Chiara), 82–83
Cologne Cathedral (Germany), 37
communion, instructions for, 110–11
Communion of Saints, 143
confession, 7–8, 102–3
    during Advent, 16
    attendance at, 7
Confessions, The (Augustine), 130
confirmandi, 60
Confirmation, 60, 65, 112
Congregation of the Mission, 134
Constantine, Saint, 130–31, 144
covenant
    between God and Abraham, 25
    continuing through David, 28–29
creation, xvii, 6, 23–24
cross, the, 85, 132, 133
crown of thorns with preserved roses, *89*

Crusades, 84
Cyril, 46

Danei, Paolo Francesco (Saint Paul of the Cross), 142
Daughters and Missionaries of Charity, 134
dayenu, 27
Dead Sea, 16
death, 72–73
Dedication of the Basilica of St. John Lateran, 144–45
Dedication of the Basilicas of Saints Peter and Paul, 145–46
desert, temptations of, 66
de Veuster, Joseph (Saint Damien of Molokai), 78, 108–9
discipleship, 97, 98–99, 100
Divine Mercy Sunday, 102–4
Dominic, Saint, 139
dominion, 24
dos Santos, Lucia, Saint, 139

Easter, 73–74, 87, 99–100
Easter Vigil, 65, 70, 71, 74, 99
Eastwood, Clint, 114
ecumenical movement, 35
Edict of Milan, 130
elect, 60
emptiness, offering up, 4
end of the world, expectation of, 62
environmentally conscious living, 53
Eucharist, 9, 10, 27, 115–16
Eucharistic Adoration, 38–39, 45
Exodus, book of, 26–28
Exposition of the Most Blessed Sacrament, 38–39
Extreme Unction, 65

faith
    growing light of, 100
    renewal of, 66–67
Faith in the Divine Initiative—the Human Response, 106
family, 126
    changes to structure of, 32, 33–34
    creating, 34

Subject/Name Index

fasting, 48, 49, 69
    during Lent, 59–60
Fatima, 107–8, 117, 139
Feast of All Saints and All Souls Day, 142–43
Feast of the Archangels, 135–36
Feast of the Ascension, 110–11
Feast of the Assumption of the Blessed Virgin Mary into Heaven, 127–28
Feast of the Baptism of the Lord, 39–41
Feast of Christ the King, 146–47
Feast of Corpus Christi, 115–16
Feast of the Epiphany, 37, 39
Feast of the Exaltation of the Holy Cross, 86, 132–33
Feast of the Holy Family, 32–34
Feast of the Holy Name of Mary, 131–32
Feast of the Immaculate Conception, 5, 9
Feast of the Immaculate Heart of Mary, 116–17
Feast of the Most Holy Trinity, 114
Feast of the Nativity of the Blessed Virgin Mary, 131–32
Feast of Our Lady of the Blessed Sacrament, 107
Feast of Our Lady of Fatima, 107–8
Feast of Our Lady of Guadalupe, 4, 5, 9
Feast of Our Lady of the Most Holy Rosary, 139–40
Feast of the Presentation of the Lord in the Temple, 43–44
Feast of the Purification of Mary, 43
Feast of the Sacred Heart of Jesus, 116–17
Feast of Saints Cyril and Methodius, 45–46
Feast of St. Alphonsus Liguori, 124–25
Feast of St. Anselm, 104–5
Feast of St. Augustine, 130–31
Feast of St. Benedict of Nursia, 120–21
Feast of St. Bonaventure, 122–23
Feast of St. Francis de Sales, 42
Feast of St. Francis of Assisi, 137–38
Feast of St. Ignatius Loyola, 124, 125–26
Feast of St. James the Greater, Apostle, 123–24
Feast of St. Joseph, 68–69
Feast of St. Joseph the Worker, 105–6
Feast of St. Luke the Evangelist, 140–41
Feast of St. Mark the Evangelist, 104–5
Feast of St. Monica, 130–31
Feast of St. Paul of the Cross, 141–42
Feast of St. Paul, 42
Feast of St. Thomas the Apostle, 119–20
Feast of St. Thomas Aquinas, 42
Feast of St. Valentine, 45–46
Feast of St. Vincent de Paul, 133–34
Feast of the Solemnity of the Blessed Virgin Mary, 36–37
Feast of Weeks, 111
fidelity, 30
First Friday Adoration, 38–39, 45, 116, 117, 125
First Luminous Mystery, 119
First Saturdays, 117
forgiveness, 8, 64
Francis of Assisi, Saint, 14, 76–87, 115, 136, 137–38
Francis and Clare (film), 85
Francis de Sales, Saint, 41–42, 136, 142
Fridays, during Lent, 48

Gabriel, Saint, 135
Gaudete Sunday, 6–8, 17, 68
Genesis, 23–24
gift giving, for Advent, 3
Giotto di Bondone, 76, 84
Glorious Mysteries, 110, 128, 139
God
    covenants of, 29
    depicted in creation stories, 23
    expulsion from company of, 24
    generosity of, 27
    as the impetus for salvation history, 103
    inviting us to the kingdom of God, 91
    of the New and Old Testaments, 29–30
    providing unity, 126–27
    relationship with Abraham, 25
    revealing himself, 103–4
    sending a new kingdom with a new king, 30–31

Subject/Name Index

Good Friday, 48, 70, 71, 74
Gospels, 140
    living the values of, 76
    new methods of experiencing, 56
    recognizing the importance of John the Baptist, 15
    responding to, in changing times, xvii–xviii
    uniqueness of each one, 90
Gubio, *138*

happiness, transmission of, 40
healing, 93–94, 141
Helena, Saint, 110, 130–31, 132, 133
Herod, 16–17
Holy Communion, presence of Christ during, 38
Holy Days of Obligation, 111, 128, 142
Holy Family, 32–34, 68–69
Holy Orders, 65
Holy Scriptures, grace of, 23
Holy Spirit, 23, 98–99, 112, 115
Holy Thursday, 70, 71, 74
Holy Week, 70, 71, 72–74
homelessness, 78–79

Ignatius of Loyola, Saint, 125–26
illness, 77–78, 92–93
immigration, 106
Incarnation, 10, 22–23, 79, 85, 122
incense, for Advent, 2
inclusive language, 78
Indian Market (Santa Fe, NM), 128–29
indulgence, 4
Innocent III, 81
institutional religions, U.S. membership in, 71
International Worker's Day, 106
Introduction to the Devout Life (Francis de Sales), 42
isolation, 99
Israel, election of, 25–26, 28–29

James the Greater, Saint, 123–24
James the Lesser, Saint, 123
January, month as month of new beginnings, 35

Jerome, Saint, 22–23, 31
Jesuit order, 125
Jesus. *See also* Christ
    Baptism of, 15–16, 39, 40, 41, 91, 98
    choosing his disciples, 96–97
    disclosed as Messiah, 92–95
    heart of, 117
    linking the Old and New Testaments, 31
    meeting personally, 55–56
    modeling behavior for Christians, 97–98
    naming of, 36
    public ministry of, 56
    presaging the priesthood of, 8
    sacred wounds of, 102
    servanthood of, 98–99
    viewed as failed Messiah, 97
John, Gospel of, 57
John the Baptist, Saint, 7, 77, 80, 91, 92, 122
    birth and life, 14–15, 118–19
    characteristics of, 19
    depictions of, 118
    Gospels recognizing the importance of, 15
    imprisonment and death of, 16–17
    ministry of, 15
    nativity of, 18, 118
John of the Cross, Saint, 142
John Paul II, 46, 102, 104, 107
Jordan River, 16
Joseph, Saint (stepfather of Jesus), 59, 60
Joyful Mysteries, 43, 139, 140
Juan Diego, Saint, 5, 9
Juliana, Saint, 115

king, role of, 29
kingdom of God, 91, 93, 96
kingdom of heaven, 146–47
Kowalska, Maria Faustina (Saint Faustina), 102, 104, 142

Laetare Sunday, 64, 67–69, 83
landscape, 52
Last Anointing, 65
Last Rites, 65

Lent, 39–40
  Advent and, 68
  almsgiving and, 62–63
  beginning of, 49
  fasting and, 59–60
  Francis of Assisi and, 77
  giving up for, 48–49
  internal signs of, 52
  learning about Francis of Assisi during, 76–87
  liturgical environment for, 54–55
  natural time to think about death, 72
  prayer for, 57–59
  reading Mark during, 90–100
  season of love, 88
  Sunday Gospels of, 56–57
  three important practices of, 48
  waiting aspect of, 51–52
lepers, 78, 79, 88, 108–9
life, creating balance in, 52–53
Life of St. Francis, The (Bonaventure), 123
Liguori, Alphonsus, Saint, 9, 38, 115, 124–25
liturgical elements, xviii, 2–3, 54–55
liturgical planning, 51
liturgical seasons
  coordinating one's actions with, xvii–xviii
  viewing as whole periods, 51
liturgical year, beginning of, 2
liturgy, 60, 64
Lord's day, keeping holy, 122–23
Lourdes, 44–45, 107
love, surrender to, 73
Luke, Saint, 140–41
Luke, Gospel of, 57, 91, 140–41
Luminous Mysteries, 40, 139

Magi, recognition of, 37
manna, 26–27
Marianne (Blessed, of Syracuse, NY), 109
Mark, Gospel of, 104–5
  as Advent Gospel, 4
  centering around Christ, 22–23
  Lenten season events in, 55
  reading during Lent, 90–100
Martin Luther King Day, 35
Mary, 140
  in Advent, 5–6
  appearing to the children at Fatima, 107–8
  Assumption of, 127–28
  beginning the transition of the tabernacle, 9
  feasts commemorating, 128
  four dogmas about, 36–37
  as human tabernacle of God, 9
  immaculate heart of, 116–17
  name of, 131, 132
  nativity of, 131–32
  as Patroness of the Americas, 5, 9, 36
  role of, in salvation history, 5–6
  seven sorrows of, 35
  speaking to the children at Fatima, 117
  titles for, 131
Mass, universality of, 51
meat, abstaining from, 48
Merton, Thomas, 74
messianic secret, 92, 94
Methodius, Saint, 46
Michael, Saint, 135
Michelangelo, 120
Mid-Lent Sunday. *See Laetare* Sunday
Million Dollar Baby (film), 114
moderation, 121
monetary worries, 27
Monica, Saint, 130–31
More, Thomas, Saint, 38
Moses, 26–27
Muslims, relations with, 84–85
Mystical Body of Christ, 126–27, 143
mystics, 141–42

National Vocations Awareness Week, 41
nativities, celebrations of, 18, 118
Nativity of Mary, 132
Nativity of St. John the Baptist, 118–19
natural world, liturgy of, 53
New Mexico, 52
New Year, 35, 36
Nouwen, Henri, 6–7
nuclear family, 33

oils, 63–66
    of the catechumens, 65
    of salvation, 65
    of the sick, 65
Old Testament
    covenants in, 30. *See also* Abraham; David
    fundamental theme of, 22
    reading as sacred history, 22
Ordinary Time, 32, 37, 39, 114, 146
original sin, 24, 53
Our Father, 77
Our Lady of Lourdes, 44–45

Palm Sunday, 69–72, 74
parables, 95–96
Paschal candle, 7, 44, 45, 61, 110
passion, 72–73
Passionists, 142
passion narrative, centrality of, 55
patience, 96
Patrick, Saint, 59–60
Paul, Saint, 122, 140, 141, 145–46
    discussing the resurrection, 55
    writings of, 42
Paul of the Cross, Saint, 141–42
Pentecost, 111–12
Perpetual Adoration, 116
Peter, Saint, 141, 145–46
Pio, Saint, 142
plenary indulgence, 103, 104
Poor Clares, 83
positive language, 78
poverty, 62–63, 79, 81
Praises of God, The (Francis of Assisi), 86
prayer, 48, 49, 69, 121
    for Lent, 57–59
    of the palms, 70–71
    types of, 43, 57–59
Prayer for Christian Unity, 35
preparation, times for, 17
Presentation of Jesus in the Temple, 43
priests, paucity of, 116
private prayer, 121
pro-life Mass, 35
public prayer, 121
purpose in life, 66–67

Raphael, Saint, 135, 136
reconciliation, 64. *See also* confession
Redepemptorist Congregation, 125
relationship, importance of, 40
repentance, 7, 8, 16
resolutions, 17, 49
resurrection, 127
Rites of Christian Initiation of Adults (RCIA), 57
Rites of Initiation, 60
rivers, 16
rosary, 36, 40, 43, 110, 119, 128, 139–40
Rose of Lima, Saint, 77
Rose Sunday. *See Laetare* Sunday
Rule, The (Benedict), 121

Sacrament of the Anointing of the Sick, 65
Sacrament of Reconciliation, 64. *See also* confession
sacraments, 8, 64
sacred, merging with the secular, xvii
sacred history, 28, 29, 30
saints, 143
salvation, Christmas and, 10
Santos, Lucia, 117
Scholastica, Saint, 121
Second Joyful Mystery, 119
secular, merging with the sacred, xvii
seeds, as metaphors for the kingdom, 96
self, death of, 73
sensus plenior, 30
Shrine of the Three Kings, 37
Sistine Chapel, 120
social sin, 53
solemnity, 37
Solemnity of Mary, 35
Solemnity of the Most Holy Body and Blood of Christ, 115–16
Solomon, 29
Sorrowful Mysteries, 139
spiritual dryness, 66–67
Spiritual Exercises (Ignatius of Loyola), 125
state of the union address, 35
Stations of the Cross, 36, 58
Stein, Edith, 46
stigmata, 85–86, 137

St. Peter's Basilica, 145
St. Vincent de Paul Society, 134
Summa Theologica (Thomas Aquinas), 41
Sunday of Refreshment. *See Laetare Sunday*
Sunday of the Five Loaves. *See Laetare Sunday*

tabernacle, 8–9
Teilhard de Chardin, Pierre, 126
Tekakwitha, Katerie (Blessed), 122–23
Ten Commandments, 8
Teresa of Avila, Saint, 142
Teresa Benedicta of the Cross, Saint (Edith Stein), 46
Teresa of Calcutta, Saint, 67
Therese of Lisieux, Saint, 77, 122
Thomas, Saint, questioning Jesus, 119–20
Thomas Aquinas, Saint, 41, 42, 115, 133, 141–42
Transfiguration of the Lord, 127
Triduum, 70, 71, 88
Trinity, 98, 114–15, 130

unity, from God, 126–27

Valentine(s), 45–46
Vatican II, 46
Vianney, John, 38
Vincent de Paul, Saint, 133–34
Visits to the Blessed Sacrament and Our Lady (Liguori), 38, 125
vocations, 116
volunteerism, 62

Week of Prayer for Christian Unity, 40
wind, 111–12, 125
work
    nature of, 121
    value of, 106
World Day of Prayer for Vocations, 105–6
World Day of the Sick, 44–45

Xavier, Francis, Saint, 38

www.ingramcontent.com/pod-product-compliance
Lightning Source LLC
Chambersburg PA
CBHW051932160426

43198CB00012B/2128